"Michael Busch is one of smartest entrepreneur's I have ever known. His knowledge of business start-ups and assessing the value of small business acquisitions is tremendous."

Barry Golin
Chicago, IL

"It is easy to see why Medicine Shoppe became so successful. Michael Busch's lessons in entrepreneurship are just outstanding."

Rachel Hyman
Raleigh, NC

"BE THE BOSS is just great. It taught me things about starting my new business that I would have never thought of. At $9.99 it is a must read."

Lauren Singer
Miami, Florida

"This is really great stuff. The material is invaluable. You cannot put a price tag on it. This is a must read for anyone thinking of buying a small business."

Jonathan Frydman
Deerfield, IL

"Michael Busch made me think twice about starting a new business and prevented me from making serious mistakes. His discussion on business planning alone is worth the price tag. His coaching really kept me focused on what I needed to do. He even prepared me for my first sit down with the bank."

Ian Broner
St. Louis, MO

mbusch.sbb@gmail.com

BE THE BOSS

HOW TO START
A NEW BUSINESS

HOW TO BUY
AN EXISTING BUSINESS

HOW TO PURCHASE
A FRANCHISE

MICHAEL BUSCH

*To JANE
Best
Michael Busch*

authorHOUSE®

AuthorHouse™
1663 Liberty Drive
Bloomington, IN 47403
www.authorhouse.com
Phone: 1-800-839-8640

Published by AuthorHouse 1/2/2013

ISBN: 978-1-4772-9656-1 (sc)
ISBN: 978-1-4772-9657-8 (e)

Library of Congress Control Number: 2012923282

Preface

Be the Boss is a compilation of lessons learned throughout my professional life. Although I've started many businesses, my greatest success was founding Medicine Shoppe International, Inc., a franchisor of more than a thousand retail pharmacies, with 2004 collective revenues in excess of $2 billion. In 1995, Cardinal Health (NYSE: CAH) acquired Medicine Shoppe in a transaction valued at approximately $360 million.

Every business I started was exactly that, a startup—and all startups are small businesses. Some grow big. Some start off with a vision to become big but never achieve it. Others simply continue to grow because they are operated correctly, have a great mission, and take on a life all their own. I've been fortunate enough to have been involved in several public offerings, all of which started as small businesses.

I have created this guide for those who want to start a new business, purchase an existing business, or buy a franchise. Each of these endeavors requires unique skills—and presents unique challenges. By following my practical recommendations, you should be able to maximize each business opportunity and reduce risk. If I'd had a book like this before starting my first business, I could have saved lots of money ... not to mention many sleepless nights!

Because most businesses involve some type of sales, I have included a section on the selling process. My sales philosophy has served me well throughout my business career. These proven principles and practical techniques can help you dramatically increase your sales.

My Background

By profession, I am a registered pharmacist, by vocation, an entrepreneur. I bought my first business in 1963, a retail pharmacy in St. Louis, Missouri. By 1968, my brother and I owned and operated four pharmacies. We had also purchased a fifth pharmacy, but sold it in less than a year. Two of the pharmacies were the inspiration for Medicine Shoppe International, Inc. In December 1968, after developing a comprehensive business plan, I successfully raised approximately $500,000 to open eight Medicine Shoppes in three different metropolitan areas. I opened these stores within a six-month period. In July, 1971 we sold the first franchise. I resigned the presidency and directorship of MSI in the mid-70's to pursue other interests. At that time, we had sold approximately 250 franchises.

My shortfall was that I was only 31 years old when I founded the company, and thought I could fly. Later, you will see how human I really was.

My career path led to many positions. These included: president of a publicly-traded tire company, VP of marketing & business development for a wholesale drug distribution company, and general manager of all non-food entities for a grocery conglomerate. I then reverted to type and became an entrepreneur once more. During this period, I started a small chain of specialty grocery stores, bought a communications consulting franchise, created a management consulting and investment banking firm for small business, and founded a turn-around consulting business. Most recently, I was a founder, chief executive officer and chairman of the board of a pharmacy data management company that was sold in 2005 to Cardinal Health, the same company that acquired Medicine Shoppe International, Inc. in 1995.

I learned many lessons from my successes–and "less than successes." (I never use the word "failure"!) But

the most important lesson was: **You must be responsible for your actions.** Most of my successes, and less than successes, were the result of my own actions. They didn't happen because I didn't have a mentor. Or because of bad weather, bad timing, or bad employees! (After all, I hired those employees.) Accepting responsibility for your actions will help you gain the most from each experience–and approach your next challenge with a positive attitude. I sincerely hope you will read this book with an open mind and use it as a blueprint for your entrepreneurial journey. It has been a privilege to share my experience with you. May it open the door to new levels of freedom and achievement in your life.

To your success!
Michael Busch

Note: If you would like additional assistance through personal business coaching, you can reach me at mbusch@bethebosstakecharge.com

Contents

Introduction

The 21st century will experience unparalleled growth in entrepreneurial business ownership. We are in the throes of a technology-driven globalization that is not only ever-changing, but promises to be central to our economic development for the foreseeable future. Gone are the days in which someone could enter into a lifelong career with one company and rely on pension benefits for a comfortable retirement. Every respected economist tells us that job creation in the U.S. will continue to come primarily from small business growth. This means that the number of people seeking "the great American dream" of owning their own business is at record levels.

This guide has been created to give you the keys to successful business ownership—and to help you reduce risk. **Owning your own business enables you to control your own destiny!** As a business owner, you are empowered to rise or fall on your own business decisions. No longer are you subjected to the whims of corporate management. No longer are decisions made by consensus of the many. No longer are you at the mercy of the next meeting or teleconference call. The success of your business lies squarely on your shoulders. As you grow and add more employees or associates, you also assume the daunting responsibility of controlling their future. It should never be forgotten that a good manager furthers the careers of his or her employees, and a bad manager puts those same people out on the street looking for jobs.

In this guide we will cover the basic principles of business formation, strategic thinking, plan execution, sales and marketing, and financing. These fundamentals will apply to any type of business you choose. We will also discuss the unique needs of new businesses, existing businesses, and franchises.

Some of you will read this and decide not to pursue business ownership. But many of you will gain renewed excitement and energy about owning your own business. Remember, every entrepreneurial venture brings stress, pressure and uncertainty. But it also brings great satisfaction, excitement and reward. I sincerely hope this guide will help you make the decision that is right for you.

There are three essential elements of success in every business. The first of these is vision. Each business owner must ask, "Where are we now, and where do we want to go?" In larger companies, the CEO is the company visionary. Every business also requires individuals capable of executing the vision. These are generally those with operational skills. Many a company with a clear vision has failed because of lack of execution. Finally, we see the need for skilled salespersons and marketers. If a company can't make the sale, there is little need for operational and technical support. In entrepreneur-owned businesses (especially startups and early stage), the owner will most likely have to provide each of these skills—and balancing them will be very challenging. For example, seldom does an experienced financial person have strong sales skills. Later on we will discuss this in greater detail and provide insight on how to compensate for deficiencies. As your business begins to grow and expand, it is essential that you match the right person to the job. Many people make the mistake of identifying a person they want to hire and then crafting the job around that person's skills and talents. This mistake has doomed many businesses.

The proper mindset significantly improves your chances of success. Knowing where you want to go is just as important as focusing on where you are. Seeing the glass as half-full and not half-empty is a must. Successful entrepreneurs don't play the "but" game (i.e., "*What a great idea, but ...*"). The "but" game is probably the greatest impediment to achieving success. It dramatically reduces your ability to make timely decisions. Remember, ***most business decisions are neither right nor wrong. It's how they turn out that matters. If you make the wrong decision, you can always take corrective action!*** But you must <u>make a decision</u>! To make no decision is the wrong decision in itself. Now let's get to it!

While much of my career centers on retail pharmacy, *Be the Boss* has been written to apply to any business. The lessons learned are applicable to most any industry. Technical aspects will differ, examples will have to be modified and the scope of the tasks outlined in various sections will need to be scaled to the size of the project. **I have seen many situations in which an applicant for a business loan provided information to the bank that far exceeded that required for the particular business. At the back of this book there is an exhibit of a Business Plan that I wrote to obtain venture capital financing in the amount of $10 million. The detail in this plan would not be applicable to financing for a $500,000 purchase of a pharmacy.**

Starting a New Business

Introspection

Do I have a vision? Do I have the skill-set to be a CEO? Can I function as the head of operations? Can I assume responsibility for sales? What about bookkeeping? Can I manage risk? How do I react to pressure and stress?

We could continue this dialogue forever, but you get my drift. Starting a new business begins with a process of self-examination. Believe it or not, few people that start businesses would do so if they knew the future. The unforeseen, the unknown, the unimaginable are the rule of thumb in every startup.

There are several essential elements that must be addressed before making the commitment. In today's rapidly changing job environment, this is even more critical. Many people are pursuing their own business as a defensive measure. These include middle-aged managers who have lost their jobs to layoffs, etc., and have minimal opportunity to find a comparable position. Therefore, it is vital to stack the deck as much as possible in favor of success.

Each of these elements is equally important.

- Do I have the support of my family?
- Are my family and I willing to make the sacrifices necessary to succeed?
- How will my family and I react to the ups and downs of running a startup?
- Do I have the ability to step outside the box and away from the insulation associated with working for a much larger company?
- Am I willing to assume total responsibility for my actions and their outcomes?
- Can I control fear?
- Am I secure enough to surround myself with individuals smarter than I?
- Do I know how to manage?
- Do I know how to delegate?
- Should I allow my spouse and/or children to be active in the business?
- How long can I survive without a paycheck?

The process of introspection or self-examination is not an easy one. It cannot be rushed and must be thorough. It must involve everyone with whom you are interdependent. To honestly identify your weaknesses as well as your strengths is most important. Success depends upon neutralizing weaknesses while enhancing strengths. For example, when I choose a new physician, the most essential qualification is that they know what they <u>don't</u> know (as opposed to what they do know). Too much ego in the medical world can cost lives. Too much ego in the business world can stifle success. This is especially true in startup businesses.

The assumption used to be that one would never start a new business without extensive experience in that field. But in today's world, many businesses are being launched by inexperienced individuals. While these persons may have had a wealth of experience in other fields, the likelihood of success in these new ventures is slim. This is especially true in the food, beverage, and entertainment businesses. The lifespan of most new restaurants is less than one year. It is a business in which you are literally as good as your last meal. Management and cost controls in any of these three sectors are more complicated and more critical than in perhaps any other industry.

However, the changing business environment will thrust more and more people into starting new businesses in which they have limited experience. And while the interest level for a particular type of business may be very high, the lack of hands-on experience will be most challenging. Yet this can be a very exciting time for those willing to move outside the box. How many of us spent years working for the "Sears & Roebuck's" of the world, believing in job security and pension benefits? In reality, business growth and job creation is going to come from entrepreneurial ownership. Remember, *every* new business is a small business. This is your time. You are reading this book because you want to experience business ownership and want to avoid as many pitfalls as you can. You may have been forced into this career path, or you may have just tired of the rat race and corporate politics. Whatever your reason, if you are cut out to be an owner, you will embark on the ride of a lifetime and most likely, never return to the past. So don't underestimate the value of personal introspection. It's the first step to becoming a successful entrepreneur.

On the other hand, don't get so caught up in introspective study that you allow it to delay a decision. Your gut feeling is critical to the process—but the decision must be made within a reasonable timeframe. Whether it is "go" or "no go," it must be made on a timely basis. Understand, I said *the decision*. Once that is made, you cannot shortchange the process of getting your business started.

Choosing a Business

Perhaps the most important step in business ownership is product selection. By that I mean choosing a business for which you are well suited. When you begin to select your business, it's important to ask yourself:

- *Am I passionate about this business?*
- *Am I being realistic about its market potential?*
- *Am I familiar with the market?*
- *Do I have any experience in this field or related fields?*
- *Can I handle the financial requirements – finance necessary growth?*
- *What is the anticipated gross margin?*
- *Is it capital intensive?*
- *Is it labor intensive? If so, what is the skill level required?*

I can't emphasize enough the value that passion adds to creating a successful business. If you aren't passionate about your business, you can hardly expect your potential customers to have passion for what you are doing. I've found that a good part of my success has been driven by involving my customers in my business. I've never failed to ask a satisfied customer for referrals. Believe me, it works!

I'm sure you're aware of this, but it's worth repeating. The highest margin businesses are service businesses, and virtually all service businesses are a form of consulting. This means that you will primarily be selling your time. These businesses have virtually no inventory and generally very few hard assets. Although this is my favorite type of business, it can have drawbacks. If you don't have any proprietary technology or systems, these businesses can be very difficult to finance. This is because there are few assets that can be used as collateral to secure either a loan or other type of investment product. It's much easier to obtain financing later on when the business cash flow has improved. I will talk more about this later.

It is very important that you do as much research as possible into your prospective industry, target market, competition, etc. The next section on business planning covers much of this in depth.

The Business Plan

Whether you are starting a new business, purchasing an existing business, or buying a franchise, you must develop a written business plan (sometimes referred to as a strategic plan). A good business plan will enable you to focus on desired outcomes and will serve as a road map for you to follow. It should be updated at least quarterly, to reflect your level of performance. Your business plan should include strategic goals and objectives to guide you from becoming a new owner to a seasoned one.

The business plan is absolutely critical to obtaining financing for your venture. This will be discussed in great detail in the chapter *"Financing Strategies."*

The business plan is critically important to those inside and outside your business. As mentioned above, it is your road map to defining operating strategies, desired outcomes, profit and loss projections, current financial information (in the case of purchasing an existing business), exit opportunities, capitalization, personnel requirements, marketing strategies, sales strategies, etc. If you intend to do any financing, gain favorable vendor terms, seek investors and/or build a banking relationship for the future, your business plan must also present you—and what you wish to accomplish—in the most favorable light.

The business plan must be compatible with your hopes and expectations. Great ideas fail due to lack of execution. In this case, you are not only the visionary, but the operator as well. As you follow the guidelines in this book, you should be able to move forward with reduced risk and greater confidence. Depending upon the size and scope of the business you intend to start, you may wish to obtain professional help to guide you in the planning process. As discussed later in the book, I am available to mentor, coach, and provide hands-on assistance in getting your business started.

My research has shown that 80% of all new businesses fail. That is eight out of every ten. One business planning service company states on their website that of 29,000 new businesses surveyed, 26,000 failed. This translates into 90%. Of these failures, 67% never had a written business plan, 57% had no outside guidance, and 71% of the owners had not taken any business courses. **I repeat, you must have a written business plan if you want to be a successful business owner.**

Creating a Business Plan

To begin with, keep it reasonably short, covering the subject matter in a concise and to-the-point manner. We all have short attention spans, and most of us do not read too much detail. Important content is best presented in the fewest possible words. It is critical that we start by developing the plan's table of contents, keeping in mind that as we prepare a business plan, we will likely insert information that will require us to change the content outline. All good business plans contain the same basics, which are then tailored to a specific business. Line up a good copy editor to ensure that your plan has correct sentence structure, spelling, and grammar. I can assure you that the very best writers when reading their works multiple times … two, three, four times … find mistakes with each reading. Here is a basic table of contents that has served me well and aided me in raising millions of dollars for new businesses.

- Executive Summary
    - Introduction
    - Value Added Proposition
    - Capital Requirements
    - Use of Proceeds
- Revenue Sources
    - Three years of Projected Revenues
- Competition
- The Market
    - Target Audience
    - Size of Market
- Marketing Plan
- Management
- Financial Plan
- Operating Plan
- Risk Analysis

Executive Summary

Introduction

The introduction is perhaps the most critical element of your plan. It should be no longer than two pages. Depending upon the business model, it could be less than a page. The first paragraph must concisely state your business's legal name and form, business purpose, and general strategy for success. Let's talk about your legal name. This is where I assert a disclaimer. I am neither an accountant nor an attorney and do not provide accounting/legal advice. Nevertheless, there are five common types of business entities: proprietorship, c-corporation, s-corporation, partnership, and limited liability corporation (LLC). Each has its own benefits and limitations, and some are better suited for certain types of businesses. By all means, obtain legal and tax accounting advice! Even if you're not ready to create the entity, you should at least have it in mind when writing your business plan. The second paragraph should identify your target customer and the size of your market.

> Example: **The Company targets an audience of the more than 35,000[1] independently owned and regional chain pharmacies accounting for 35% of the total market. Collectively, they maintain a detailed patient database of more than 135 million lives. 1999 total industry Rx revenues of $120 billion are expected to double, generating $240 billion by 2005.**

In the example above, the emphasis is on collecting accurate facts and statistics. It is not sufficient to guess at the market size; you have to back it up with legitimate documentation (in this case, with a footnote).

Whether we are talking about opening a restaurant, manufacturing facility, or consulting practice, the Introduction contains the same type of information, tailored to each business.

It is very important that you avoid words that are superlative in nature (e.g., *superb* skills, *outstanding* marketing strategy). You should also refrain from minimizing your goals and objectives. Many business plans make this mistake by using the word "conservative" (e.g., *"The financial projections are a conservative estimate"*; *"The stated results from our marketing plan are very conservative"*). **No! No! No!** Investors or lenders will form their own opinions as to how aggressive or conservative your projections are. Lenders and investors will discount your projections regardless of where they fall. This is just the way it is. So if you try to direct their thinking by use of words, you do yourself a great disservice and may totally turn off the reader.

Value Added or Unique Proposition

What is unique about or provides added value to your business model? In business terms, this quality is called a "value added" or "unique" proposition. At the time I created Medicine Shoppe International, Inc. I operated one pharmacy that was a pseudo-prototype

---

1   National Community Pharmacists Association (NCPA) June 22, 1999

of what I wanted our Medicine Shoppes to be. I say pseudo because the only thing they were going to have in common was the business model. The new stores were going to look totally different. The value added or unique proposition was that I developed a low-entry investment model that could compete with major chains like Walgreens. Because Medicine Shoppes limited their services to prescriptions and related items, we were able to offer an affordable investment product to pharmacists who wanted ownership—or pharmacy owners looking for an expansion vehicle. ***In short, the value added proposition was that we were selling a system of doing business.*** So-called industry experts told me that we could never sell a franchise to a pharmacist who was "professionally qualified" to open and operate a pharmacy. Nevertheless, at its optimum there were over 1,200 Medicine Shoppes operating internationally as far away as India and Taiwan.

Here is another example. Several years ago, I raised $750,000 for a client who wanted to open a flower shop in a major indoor mall location. I succeeded in doing this because I recognized a unique proposition in his business plan. This unique proposition was that we were not in the business of selling flowers or floral accessories. We were in the business of making people feel better(by celebrating special occasions or providing comfort during illness). Therefore, we were competing with the bookstore, liquor store, candy shop, gift shop, etc. ***By understanding this, we taught a whole different method of selling our products, and that was the "value added" proposition.*** I will discuss this in greater detail in the section on competition, and again in the section on selling.

The following is an excerpt from the business plan of a B2B (Business to Business) company in the throes of raising venture capital during the dot.com era. This business plan is provided to you in its entirety as an exhibit in the back of the book. But this shows you how this company describes its value added proposition.

"The Company believes it will achieve a market share of eight percent or 3,000 ASP users by the end of Year Two and a fifteen percent market share representing 5,400 users by the end of Year Three. The Company outlines the value added propositions supporting this projection below.

- *Electronic linkage in the pharmacy value chain is a foregone conclusion. Pharmaceutical manufacturers, patients, physicians, pharmacies, PBMs (Pharmacy Benefit Managers) and Managed Care Organizations (MCOs) will all be part of the link. Independent retail pharmacies and smaller chains must opt to participate in the company's program or a similar model or risk exclusion from participation.*

- *The Company enables the pharmacies to keep pace with burgeoning prescription growth by providing the stores with its three-part outside pharmacy fulfillment program, mitigating the stores' need for additional capital requirement while increasing store profits.*

- *While all B2B solutions can add value, B2B companies incur high marketing costs to attract "eyeballs." The Company provides connectivity to its target audience, the pharmacy community. Its ASP applications zero in on tools to enable its participating pharmacies to grow market share without a corresponding proportionate investment."*

Although this business plan detailed only a concept and vision, with the technology still in development, we were able to obtain a $10 million venture capital commitment. My associates and I envisioned building a business that five years down the road would have a market capitalization of somewhere between $300 and $500 million dollars. **But it was not to be!** Along came the dot.com bust and the venture capital companies were up to their ears in huge investment losses. Most decided to eliminate new investments except in those ventures that they believed could be saved.

Only months before, these same venture capitalists were throwing money at startup dot. coms as fast as the startups could absorb the capital.

While we had a good initial plan, we had to retool the company into a less aggressive business model because of this economic downturn. We were also forced to partner with a prominent NYSE-listed technology company in order to acquire necessary capital to continue the business. In the fall of 2005, we sold the business assets of the company to one of the leading pharmaceutical distribution companies in the country—for significantly less than the $300 million we had anticipated.

I share this with you because I believe it is a good example of how to describe the value added proposition of a business. There must be real substance that will differentiate you from the other guy. In addition, this is one of my entrepreneurial enterprises where we did not achieve the successful outcome that we anticipated. We survived, but we did not win. We did, however, get lots of education! The $10 million commitment was lost in 24 hours. Until the money is in the bank, there is no commitment. Whether you are seeking $200,000 for your business or $10 million, each is proportionately relative to future success and ability to operate. Therefore, the same thought process must apply.

It is very important to identify the special value added proposition because it will help you to focus your operating plan on the essential elements to achieve success. The right focus will keep you in control and enable you to prepare for the inevitable: *adverse conditions over which you have no control.*

I am reminded of the time I visited two men's clothing stores on the same day that were two blocks apart. I asked the first owner how business was for the week and he responded that volume was down because the weather was bad and nobody was coming out to shop. A short while later I asked the second owner the same question. His response was the exact opposite. Because the weather was so poor, people had nothing else to do but shop. There are two lessons to be learned here. The first is if you are a "glass half-empty" kind of person, the glass will never have a chance to be full. The second lesson is that there are many things in business that are beyond human control (weather being one of them). It's obvious the second owner refused to use the weather as an excuse and was determined to do business in spite of it. The primary difference between these two owners is that the latter had identified his value added proposition.

Capital Requirements

I believe that you should put your capital requirements right up front as part of your Executive Summary. Any financing source wants to know the bottom line: the required amount, structure, term etc. If you are asking for an equity investment, then you have to be prepared to discuss what you are willing to give up in terms of ownership. This is tailored to the type of financing that you are seeking. The section on financing will help you understand how to word this in your business plan. Also, the exhibits in the back of this book will provide you with real world examples.

You must also discuss your capital contribution to the business. Any personal effort beyond your capital inclusion is deemed "sweat equity." When dealing with equity investors, be careful not to place too much–or too little–value on this subjective variable.

Use of Proceeds

In "Capital Requirements," we tell the investor audience what our needs are and specifically how the capital is going to be used. One word of caution: you must provide for sufficient working capital when discussing your capital requirements and use of proceeds.

Example of Capital Requirement Section of the Business Plan

JVC Corporation is seeking $400,000 in debt financing to support an equity investment of $150,000. Collateral will consist of all tangible assets and intangible assets of the business.

Use of Proceeds:
Inventory...............$250,000.00
Equipment............ 100,000.00
Furniture.............. 25,000.00
Working Capital..... 175,000.00

Total Proceeds........$550,000.00

Revenue Sources

In this section of the business plan, you must identify how primary revenues will be generated. It is essential to include:

- Each source of revenue and the price of each service or product you offer
- The size of your target audience
- Anticipated volume relative to the market
- Competitive positioning in your pricing strategies
- Projected sources of future revenue

A word of caution on the last item: Don't identify future revenue sources if they require additional investments.

This section is not your financial plan. Depending upon your business, it may be very short and to the point. In the case of the ASP B2B plan I described above, the Revenue Sources section totaled seven and a half pages, with some charts and assumptions. However, if you were starting an automotive repair shop, you would identify revenue from the various categories of repair and service; in a retail store, you would define by categories of goods and also address the profit margin of each element of revenue. It is likely that in either of these cases, fewer pages would be required. In any event, using a table to reflect revenues for the next three to four years is very helpful. The first year may be a partial year (i.e. if your business begins operations in June, the first year will be for six months). This enables you to use calendar years for the next three years.

Let's pause here and take a deep breath. I want you to know that you have the desire, drive, basic resources, and skills to own and operate your business. The fact that you chose to purchase this guide tells me that you have the drive to change your life and expand your knowledge. This guide will give you all of the information you need to go forward. You will know what resources you will need, where to find them, and how to best use them. Most important, your confidence level will rise and apprehensions will diminish. **Please do not let anything that we talk about overwhelm you. It will all come together.** Should you need additional assistance in moving your new venture along, remember that I am available to coach you on a one-on-one basis.

Competition

I cannot emphasize enough the need to carefully study your competition. Competition may well dictate much of your operating strategy. The depth and breadth of your competitors will dictate how aggressive your operating plan can be. It is very important to think through the consequences of your operating and marketing strategies so that you can anticipate competitor reaction. **Never operate blindly.** You should not be obsessed with your competition, but should always be well versed in how they operate their businesses. Expand upon what they do right and learn from what they do wrong.

Another thing to remember: **Good competition benefits your business, while bad competition hurts you**. And no competition at all tells me that the new business venture is likely to be ahead of its time. There are advantages and disadvantages to being first in the marketplace. The main advantage is that as long as you remain creative, the other players have to play "catch up." Conversely, being first typically requires longer staying power because you are paving new ground. Also, you may open the door for the competitor with more resources, making it more expensive for you to stay in the game. A great example of this was Netscape. According to Tom Friedman's *The World is Flat*, Netscape drove Internet communications to a whole different level and likely was the greatest influence on where we are today. But, lo and behold, along came Microsoft. Because of the impact of its operating system technology, Microsoft was able to give away that for which Netscape had to continue to charge. Don't you think this adversely impacted Netscape's value? But, I wouldn't cry too much for John Barksdale, one of Netscape's founders and leader. He literally changed the world for the better and achieved that of which most of us only dream.

Here are some examples of where defining and understanding your competition correctly can make the difference between success and lessons learned the hard way. Many years ago, I became aware of a company out of Germany that came to the United States to open a unique kind of grocery store. The stores were named Aldi—maybe you are familiar with them. Their concept was to buy only promotional items, predominately dry groceries, as opposed to produce and meats. Products would be stacked on the floor in original cases, price signs above the product, but nothing individually priced. Cashiers also memorized merchandise prices. All of these strategies significantly reduced labor and technology costs below those of conventional supermarkets.

I proceeded to put some investment capital together and opened several "Super Cheap" Food Stores, one in Pittsburgh and another in Sharon, Pennsylvania. I retained an advertising agency and they developed a logo of a yellow canary in a Superman costume saying, **"Cheap..Cheap..Cheap!"**

During the grand opening of the first store in a section of Pittsburgh called East Liberty, the store's gross revenue the first day was more than $15,000. The lines outside the store required policemen to direct traffic. However, three things occurred that ultimately doomed us to failure. The first was that one of our investors knew the Chairman and CEO of Pittsburgh's largest supermarket chain. Well, about a month after our great opening, the investor (who shall remain nameless) decided to brag about his investment in Super Cheap Food Stores and how the company was going to really give the chain supermarkets a "run for their money." This simple conversation doomed our plan which was to quickly and strategically place three to five stores in Pittsburgh suburbs to defray the cost of advertising and gain publicity. My hope was that we might attract a buyer for the company from one of the supermarket chains. Instead, all desirable locations were suddenly unavailable. Shopping center owners were reluctant to do business with this upstart new company at the risk of alienating the chain supermarket industry (which, in many cases, anchored the shopping center).

The second mistake was mine. I was determined to open another store at all costs. So I decided to go outside Pittsburgh to Sharon, PA. It soon became apparent that I did not have a strong enough management team to be able to operate stores in two different markets. Remember, I was not a grocery guy and although I had worked for a supermarket conglomerate, my expertise was in non-foods.

My third mistake was that I underestimated my competition. The store was opened next door to a national chain supermarket. As soon as we began advertising our grand opening, the competition began to match every price. Now this is called predatory pricing and is, in fact, a restraint of trade violation. You see, the chain was legally bound to have all of its stores within the same geographic marketing area sell at the same prices. Only they did not do this. Instead they took the one store next door and applied predatory pricing. Of course my next course of action was to consult with a prominent Pittsburgh law firm. I received good and bad news. We had a classic "David vs. Goliath" case. However, it would likely take five years to reach conclusion and we could expect to have legal fees in the mid-six figures. Six months later, Super Cheap filed for Chapter 11 under the bankruptcy act; and shortly thereafter, it was liquidated. The bottom line: Anticipate the competition's reaction and never let ego (yours or your investor's) do you in.

Notwithstanding the lessons learned above, here is an example of successfully identifying and understanding competition. Earlier I told you a little about the florist that I was able to assist in raising capital. The business was owned and operated by a husband-and-wife team. Capital was needed to open a second shop in a major downtown mall. The great advantage this company had was product selection. Because they consistently imported flowers from South America, they offered a variety that few, if any, of their competitors could match. However, I believed that they were limited in growth due to a lack of understanding of the real definition of their business. You will soon see what I mean.

The company employed approximately 12 full-time and part-time sales and design associates, and the owners decided to retain my firm to provide sales training. This is where we were able to make the greatest impact on the company's growth. I began the training by asking each associate (including the owners) to briefly describe what business they were in. The first said, *"Oh, we sell flowers."* The next said, *"We sell flowers and floral accessories."* And each description was the same, with minor variations. All of these individuals believed that the purpose of their business was to sell flowers, plants, accessories, etc.

Prior to beginning this training, I gave a lot of thought to what I knew about the flower business. And I came to some interesting conclusions. There were fundamentally two types of customers, one who sends flowers to someone else (e.g., as a get-well gesture, for a special occasion, to a spouse, etc.). The second type of customer is the individual who purchases flowers for themselves. Before we discuss the characteristics of each of these customers, allow me to digress. I also discovered that typically when I call a florist to place an order, the very first question I get is *"How much do you want to spend?"*

Let's take the customer who is sending flowers to a friend in the hospital. If you were this customer, wouldn't you want your flowers to be the very best that the person receives? I certainly would. Therefore, I taught the sales associates to *never* ask the customer how much they want to spend. Instead, the dialogue should go like this:

> **Customer: *"I want to send flowers to my aunt who is in the hospital"***
>
> **Sales Associate: *"Well I can give you a wonderful arrangement of reds, yellows, greens, purples, just an exciting and beautiful floral arrangement."***
>
> **Customer: *"That sounds great, but how much is it?"***
>
> **Sales Associate: *"We can give you this for $75.00".***
>
> **Customer: *"Oh! I only wanted to spend $60.00. What can you give me for that amount?"***
>
> **Sales Associate: *"Not to worry! I can give you yellows, greens, purple, whites....it will be gorgeous, I promise!"***

You get the point. Never once in that exchange did the sales associate ask the customer what they wanted to spend. But the results were win-win because the customer believed that she was sending a knock-out arrangement, and in many cases, she may well have gone with the $75.00 arrangement. If someone were to ask me how much I wanted to spend, I would answer by saying the least amount I can for the most that I can get.

Now, let's take the customer who is buying flowers for themselves. It is Friday evening, and a woman comes into the shop looking to buy flowers. What could this tell us?
- She doesn't have a date and is looking to give herself some cheer.
- She is having dinner guests and is splurging for some flowers.
- She wants to put some joy into her house.

In any case, the flower shop is competing with a variety of other possible product purchases (e.g., a book, bottle of wine, tickets for a play, etc.) By recognizing who your competition is, your sales presentation totally changes. Do you have any doubts that the florist armed with this knowledge is going to out-perform the conventional florist and provide much greater value to its customer?

I give you these examples because I want you to think outside the box. Anyone can write a business plan. There are many so-called business gurus that can advise you and provide you with a table of contents for your plan.

However, I believe that you must emotionally and intellectually understand what your business is about. It will lead to more realistic expectations and certainly help to define that "value added proposition" that I spent so much time talking about.

If I do nothing else for you, I want to provide a comfort level that lets you know that you are approaching this new business venture, or even your existing early-stage business, in a manner that will give you potential for the greatest upside.

The Market

Here is where you describe your target market as specifically as possible, including size and location. To add credibility to your market profile, I recommend using the most accurate and current statistics available. This is especially important when seeking outside financing. And don't forget to footnote all of your data sources.

Market Analysis Example

The primary business market is measured by a 5-mile radius of the store. The following statistics apply:

- *Population: 250,000*
- *Households: 80,600*
- *Median Household Income: $48,380*
- *Drive-by Traffic Counts: 7,050 cars (24-hour period)*
- *Walk-by Traffic Counts: N/A*
- *Competitors: Primary – 3; Secondary - 1*

Marketing Plan

This is where you begin to dissect your target audience and describe exactly how you intend to reach it. Although each business will require its own specific solutions, no business can survive by just waiting for the customer to show up. Therefore, it is essential to develop a marketing strategy that meets both your unique business needs and budget.

I want to emphasize that not everything in your strategy will work and your financial planning must take this into consideration. In this section, we will discuss the "why's" and "why not's."

In the planning process, it is critical to realistically determine the size and location of your market, various ways to reach your market, marketing-related investment requirements, and the risk/reward ratio for each marketing endeavor.

It's also critically important to review your competition's advertising and marketing efforts. There's no reason to reinvent the wheel. What you want to do is to take the best of what competitors do, eliminate the worst, and try to enhance what is already successful.

Marketing may consist of the following:

- Collateral material – brochures, direct mail pieces, shelf-talkers, etc.
- Public Relations – press releases, media stories, unsolicited testimonials, community participation, etc.
- Advertising – print, broadcast, direct mail, web

It is essential that you track responses to each advertising and marketing endeavor. Because marketing success is gained by trial and error, we repeat what works and eliminate what doesn't. The more specifically you can target your customer, the greater the response—and lower the selling cost. Successful marketing is usually a direct result of how effectively you track, and then measure, the cost versus the result. I tend to look at every expense in terms of risk versus reward. If the risks outweigh the potential reward, I do not pursue. Here is a clear example of what I mean. I used to like to visit casinos on occasion. But as of late, I steer clear of them. Why? It hurts more to lose $1,000 than to have a chance to win $5,000. The win, if it occurs, does not really affect my life, while the loss is a cost that will bother me.

There are many creative ways to grow a business and increase customer count—and some are even free! Here are a couple of my favorites.

Example 1
I was speaking before a student audience of over 100 attendees and asked the following question. ***Can anyone tell me how you can create a national image for a retail business with only one or two stores?*** No one volunteered an answer. I then related how I was able to accomplish giving our first Medicine Shoppe pharmacy in Nashville, TN a national image.

I created the Medicine Shoppe National Guarantee of Benefits for enrolled customers. One of the benefits was: *"If traveling anywhere in the United States and you need your medicine refilled, simply go to any Medicine Shoppe and they will promptly refill your prescription. However, if there is not a convenient Medicine Shoppe nearby, simply go to any pharmacy. Your Medicine Shoppe back home will refund you any long distance charges you incurred with the other pharmacy and in the event that pharmacy charged you a higher price for your medication, your Medicine Shoppe will gladly refund you the difference."* This one benefit created a national image in the mind of the customer.

Example 2

Many years ago I took a furniture company nationwide by developing a franchise program. The company was called "Naked Furniture," and primarily sold unfinished furniture. I was visiting a franchise in Michigan and over lunch I asked the owner-operator how business was. He said that it was spotty. I then asked him how many customers he had telephoned the previous day. A puzzled look crossed his face. When we returned to the store, I asked to look at the receipts for the previous day's business. It seems that Mrs. Jones purchased a dining room table and six chairs for $2,250. My next step was to call her. *"Mrs. Jones, this is Michael Busch at Naked Furniture. I'm sorry to bother you, but I had to call you right away. We were reviewing our sales yesterday and it came to my attention that we overcharged you $3.75. I know it's not a big amount but still it is a mistake. Next time you're in the store, please pick up an envelope at the register with your money. Also, I am including a $25 gift certificate for putting you to this trouble. Thanks. Oh! By the way, how do you like the dining room furniture? Great! Again, thank you for being so understanding."*

When I hung up the phone, the store owner asked me what I thought would happen. After giving him the money for the customer, I replied that I didn't have the faintest idea, but that I wanted him to call me whenever she returned to pick up the envelope. A few weeks later he called sheepishly to tell me that Mrs. Jones came in and brought her neighbor Mrs. Smith who had never been to the store. Mrs. Smith purchase was $7,340. **I would stand outside the store everyday giving out $3.75 to get a Mrs. Smith!** Creativity and imagination are essential elements to effective selling.

Example 3

I went to visit my friend, George, who owned a high-volume retail drugstore and told him that I wanted to try an experiment. For the next 30 days, I wanted each of his pharmacists and technicians to randomly call customers. I gave him two examples:

"Hi Mrs. Smith, this is George at ABC Drugs. How are you today? I'm glad to hear it. I'm calling because I haven't seen you or Mr. Smith lately, and I just wanted to make sure everything is okay. Well, that's great. Oh and how is Amy? Is she selling Girl Scout cookies this year? Well, tell her to be sure and see me for my order. Thanks, it was good to talk to you."

"Hi Mrs. Jones, this is George at ABC Drugs. I see where Sally got a prescription yesterday for an antibiotic. Is the medication beginning to work? Is she feeling better? That's great. Well, I just wanted to check up and see how Sally was feeling. See you soon. Goodbye."

I then asked George to do one more thing. I asked him to have his checkout personnel ask every new customer this question: ***"By the way, do you get your prescriptions filled here? You don't? Let me introduce you to George, our chief pharmacist. George, can you come over here for a minute. George, this is a new customer, and I wanted you to meet him."***

During the next 30 days, ABC Drugs gained 15 new prescription customers. Over the course of one year, ABC's business also increased by $500,000. Part of this was due to price increases. But much of it was the direct result of word-of-mouth sales and improved customer relations. Best of all, it didn't cost George a penny to market this way!

The lesson here is that you can do many things to help your business grow. These techniques are not industry–specific and will give you a unique selling proposition. I assure you that most businesses have never even thought of this selling strategy. It continues to amaze me how businesses spend millions of dollars on advertising and don't even think about improving customer service and building customer relations.

Okay! That's enough anecdotes for now. Let's get back to conventional marketing. It's very important that you know your desired outcome for each of your marketing and advertising strategies. And it's doubly important that your expectations are realistic. For example, if you create a brochure, the best you can hope for as a desired outcome is to obtain an inquiry. This is because brochures don't actually sell anything. If properly designed, they are only intended to pique curiosity, which may eventually lead to a sale.

If we take a good look at all marketing and advertising venues, we need to make sure that each thing we do has one common thread: a call to action. We must ask the viewer to *do* something. If your business is going to have a website, then all other mediums that you use should emphatically direct the viewer or reader to your website. Why? Because it's more affordable and accessible than other mediums, you can tell your story much better on your website than anywhere else. This is why a classified ad that simply directs someone to your website may yield surprisingly high dividends.

What about a website? How do I design it? How do I get traffic to it? Believe it or not, most websites are not as effective as they could be. There are many do's and don'ts associated with successful web marketing. I will cover some of them here. However, if you are interested in starting a web-based business, I will tell you later how to obtain an excellent course on the subject.The Internet is full of people who want to build your website. Sadly, most are designers and not marketers. While most businesses have a website for professional credibility, not all are taking full advantage of this excellent marketing tool. If you want to attract visitors to your site and convert them to customers, here are some important tips.

- **Call to action** - Every page of your site must direct the visitor to take action, even if that action is directing the person to go to another page. If you are selling something, it's important to ask for the order in several places on your site. At the very least, you want to direct the visitor to a response form where they supply you with name, address, email address, etc. The more information you can get, the better. One way to obtain this is to provide something free in exchange for their contact info. Every visitor is an important lead, so you must be able to reach him!

- **Site Structure** – All pages should contain navigation links to every page in your site. These links should appear on the top and bottom of each page. Most sites typically include the following pages: Home – The first page of your site should welcome prospective customers and give them an overview of your business. It should also direct visitors to take a specific action; otherwise, they may leave your site.

  1. About us – Information on your company, its management, etc. Testimonials – Include several to give your business credibility.

  2. Contact us – This is where you furnish your address, email address, telephone and name of person to be contacted.

  3. News and Events – Contains the latest information about your business, such as new products/services or awards. May also include notice of special events.

  4. Order Now – Enables visitors to order your product or service at any time.

  5. Links or Affiliate Sites – This is a form of cross-marketing, where other sites with which you have agreed to "trade links" are available to give your site visitors direct access to related products.

- **Download Time** – I recommend that you refrain from excessive animation and graphics, which simply slow down your site. Ideally, visitors should be able to access each site page within 1 – 2 seconds for broadband and within 5 – 7 seconds for dial-up service.

- **Professional Service** – The great advantage to having a website is its economic value. You could never afford to provide all that is contained in your site in other media. Later, I will provide contact info for several competent web designer/marketers. The extra cost for professional service is well worth the results. After all, you can have the greatest site, but if there is no traffic, you will have wasted time and money.

- **Search Engines** – A successful website is usually one that targets a niche market rather than trying to reach everyone. Professional web marketers will also be able to ensure that your prospective customers can easily find your site. This is done by seamlessly adding strategically selected search phrases–called "keywords"–to your website. If you found your way to www. SHBConsultants.com through a search engine, you probably used a keyword that took you to my site.

Management

This is really self-explanatory. The key members of your team are described in this section. One note of caution: Don't make it a resume. Degrees are only important if they are relevant to the position. For example, a medical company would want to emphasize that the owner is an MD.

This is an opportunity to toot your company's horn. If you need to seek financing, investors or lenders will place much weight on the quality of your management team. When describing their qualifications, be sure to point out specifically how their experience will benefit your company (rather than just listing their achievements).

Financial Plan

This is commonly referred to as the "make or break section" of your business plan. Whether you are buying an existing business or starting a new one, you must have a financial plan.

If you are buying an existing business, you should look at a minimum of three years of financial statements—in as much detail as possible. This includes balance sheets, income statements, cash flow statements (if available) and income tax returns.

Whether you are buying or starting anew, you need to put together three years of pro forma financial statements. The reason I use three years is because forecasting five years out is just not practical or believable. This is based upon your operating plan. The operating plan is the narrative behind the financial projections that tells you how you intend to achieve your numbers.

I suggest that you put your financials on an Excel spreadsheet for ease of use. All three years should be projected on a month-by-month format and consolidated at the end (balance sheet, income statement and statement of cash flow). It's important that your month-by-month projections take into account seasonality of the business. You can't just take a 12-month revenue projection and divide by 12. Also, in preparing assumptions, it's wise to divide your expenses into fixed and variable categories. Fixed expenses are just that, expenses that your business incurs every month regardless of revenue generated. Variable expenses are directly related to revenue, which varies each month. At the beginning of this section, I suggested that you provide your assumptions and consolidated projections for each of the three years in a table format. The detailed pro forma will follow. As a side note, I always do a number of rewrites on financial projections, increasing expenses and reducing revenue each time. This practice can help you avoid the number one cause of new business failure: Under-capitalization. Remember, don't use the word "conservative" in your narrative. Your projections are supposed to be *realistic*, not liberal or conservative.

This leads to something else. You need to do a little research to learn industry norms for rent, salaries, marketing/advertising, selling costs, etc. The more you are within these norms, the greater the chance of success. If you have a unique product, you may need to spend more on marketing/advertising to educate the consumer. Your budget should always include your salary. Investors or lenders will be suspicious if you don't intend to take a salary. Your salary will most likely be tied to the amount of invested capital you provide. The greater the outside financing, the more "sweat equity" you will have to contribute. This isn't always the case, but keep it in the back of your mind. I suggest you involve your accountant in laying out your projections. However, you will need to give him or her some direction, especially if they don't have a strong background in your specific business. Obviously, if you can find an accountant or bookkeeper with experience in your business, this is a great advantage.

When developing your projections, you should also be aware of the importance of timing.

For example, if your business plan is based on beginning operations in June, then your first year of projections should show six months of performance (June through December). This allows you to include three years of additional projections based on the calendar year, January through December.

Also, when you prepare monthly income projections, you should provide the most detail possible. For example, if you derive revenue from three different sources, you need to line-item each source. On the expense side, you should use as much detail as is practical. Your miscellaneous expense category should be very small. Think of this exercise as being no different than preparing your budget at home. You break out things such as rent/mortgage payment, utilities, telephone, lawn service, etc. It's no different in business. Think of your projections as your budget. Not being specific enough can hurt in two ways. First, it hampers your using the projections as a meaningful benchmark to measure performance. Second, if you are using the projections to raise investment capital—or to obtain a loan—and don't provide sufficient data, you will turn off anyone who reads your business plan. Every potential lender or investor performs due diligence before making a decision. It only stands to reason, that they will expect you to do the same. **Most investors are investing in *you*. The more thoroughly you prepare your financial plan—and the better you present it—the better your chances of securing capital.**

For most, creating a financial plan is foreign and, thus, difficult. To help you, I have included a simple financial plan in the Exhibits section at the end of this book. I am also available to provide additional assistance as needed. Generally, when I prepare financial projections, I create as many as five or six different scenarios. In each subsequent set, I lower revenue expectations and increase costs.

A word to the wise: Make sure you check your math over and over again. There is nothing worse than providing inaccurate financials. You should also have someone edit your grammar and punctuation. Accuracy is essential.

Finally, I want to emphasize that every business must keep pace with its growth. The healthy growth of your business depends upon your ability to finance that growth. Without the necessary capital, many a worthy business is driven into oblivion.

The Financial plan must include projected (i) Balance Sheets; (ii) Income Statements; (iii) Statements of Cash Flow.

Operating Plan

Well, you have spent countless hours putting together three+ years of financial projections. If you are anything like me, you did the numbers over and over until you were seeing numbers in your sleep. Obviously, the projections didn't just drop out of the sky. There had to be a basis for determining revenues, expenses, investment cost, cash flow, etc. **That basis is your operating plan!**

The operating plan can best be described as the narrative to your financial plan. It should fully explain how you are going to run your business. This includes everything from hours of operation and implementation of marketing strategies to addition of personnel. It should also describe exactly who is responsible and accountable for what. In many business plans, this is the section where flowcharts and organizational charts are used. However, the extent to which you use charts, ratios, graphs and tables should be directly related to the complexity of your business. The more complex and detailed your business plan, the more need for these "picture tools."

Your operating plan should be your guide to the daily operation of your business. Whenever you need to change your systems or procedures, simply update your business plan. Think of it as a living document, subject to change as you go through the trials and errors of running a new business.

Risk Analysis

There are risks associated with your business, right? Well, believe me, investors and bankers are very much aware of these risks. That's why it's important for you to address them right away. Most people will shy away from talking about risk, believing that negativity affects their plan. On the contrary, it's probably the single most important factor in establishing your credibility. Jump right in and identify the risk – then explain your solution for reducing it. A risk analysis may take on many shapes and forms. It can include anything from a discussion of the seasonality of your business to reviewing an industry shortage of qualified personnel. If you are buying an existing business, one of the risk factors may well be an initial attrition of customers. The risks are real, and you have to have a solution to reduce or eliminate them.

In many ways, this is the most important part of your business plan. Everyone will discount your projections. In fact, even you should discount them. It is rare for someone to exceed their projections, and most people don't achieve them in the allotted time. This is especially true for startup businesses. By owning up to the risks and providing realistic strategies to overcome them, you take them off the table. They no longer are the first line of defense of a skeptical or reluctant investor/lender.

Business Formation

As your pharmacy business grows and changes, you may find that you need to change the legal entity in which you operate. Please note we are not accountants or attorneys. Thus, we strongly recommend that you seek professional advice before deciding if and when you need a change. The following are simple definitions to get you started.

Proprietorship
By definition, a proprietorship is individual ownership d/b/a (doing business as). A proprietorship requires the least legal assistance in formation and is the least expensive structure to maintain. There is one drawback. Any liability associated with your business becomes your personal liability.

C-Corporation
A C-Corporation is the most common legal entity for fairly substantial size corporations (multiple stockholders). It provides insulation from personal liability except in cases where the principal owner has provided personal guarantees. The corporation files income taxes and is taxed on company profits. All employees, including the principal owner, must be salaried in order to take money from the company. Otherwise, all revenue going to management and shareholders would be considered dividend income subject to double taxation (first to the company and then to the individuals receiving dividend income).

S-Corporation
An S-Corporation has the same corporate characteristics, regarding liability issues, as the C-Corporation. But it functions like a proprietorship, where income distribution is concerned. The "S-Corp" is required to file a corporate tax return; however, income (or losses) flow directly through to the shareholders, on a pro-rated basis, as personal income (or loss). Thus, the corporation itself is not taxed.

Limited Liability Corporation or LLC
Instead of stockholders, the LLC has members. Its characteristics are similar to that of a partnership; however, it may have a bit more insulation from individual liabilities for its manager.

Partnership
A Partnership is similar to an LLC, in that it has a general partner (active in the business) and may contain passive investors.

There is some flexibility in your business structure selection. For example, you can go from operating as a proprietorship to operating as a corporation. There are also mechanisms that will allow you to elect to change from a C-Corporation to an S-Corporation, or the reverse. Generally, you can only change your mind one time. Once again, we encourage you to seek professional help in determining which option is best for you.

Legal and Accounting

One of the many lessons I've learned the hard way is that a number of risks associated with starting a new business can be reduced by choosing the right professionals to help you. You should begin by determining what you want from your legal and financial advisors, not just today, but down the road as your business grows. After some initial mistakes, I began to seek out professionals who were experienced in startup businesses, but could also share my vision of the future. For the most part, I tried to avoid big law and accounting firms because I didn't want to pay for their interns' mistakes.

This is not to say that large firms don't have their strengths. Certainly, they have greater resources, but they also charge more. I recently did a transaction with a major New York Stock Exchange listed company. Their in-house counsel (lawyers working for the company) spent countless hours on what was essentially a very small transaction in relation to its size. I'll bet the costs associated with its large Wall Street-type outside law firm exceeded $150,000. My legal fees were less than $6,000. Worst of all, it took almost six months to complete a transaction that easily could have been done in 30 days.

I also try to seek counsel from those who have some knowledge of my business industry. For example, a real estate attorney is of little help to me if my business is in the retail sector. He or she may be able to advise me on business formation but will most likely not benefit me as I try to grow the business. Also, bear in mind that you know your business better than your professionals and are fully invested in it. Follow your instincts. Don't give any control to either your accountant or attorney—and do your best to limit the costs associated with their work on your behalf.

Exit Strategies

An exit strategy is defined as a plan to maximize the return on your investment if and when you decide to leave the business!

Here is where I may put a damper on your enthusiasm for starting a new business. This is especially true for those who are considering the entrepreneurial route due to unemployment. I single you out because it's easy to make the decision to start or buy a business in order to buy yourself a job. But people with this mindset generally fare poorly at business ownership. This is because owning a business typically requires an investment, and an owner's primary focus should be on generating a return on that investment. This goes beyond simply being compensated for your time, as with a job.

The return on your investment (ROI) can come from different actions. Before starting your business, you should formulate the various ways in which you can achieve this ROI. Here are some general scenarios that may or may not relate to your business.

- The business generates annuity-like returns. In this case, you may not need an exit strategy—especially if the revenue will continue to flow even upon retirement or death.

- The business is such that the real wealth will be created after you grow to a certain level and sell the business. In this scenario, you should identify your potential buyer(s) up front, if at all possible.

- The business is expected to offer the potential of selling off equity. You may sell equity either privately or in the public arena. However, if you sell equity privately, you will most likely need an exit strategy for your investors—as well as one for yourself.

- The business has refinancing value.This is especially true if your business is buying and selling commercial real estate. As you add value to your property, you can refinance and take capital out.

- The business lends itself to an employee buyout. This means that you have built a business, and your exit is selling to your employees. One word of caution: Make sure that they contribute capital to the transaction with full knowledge that you may have to finance part of it. In this case, be sure your employees are financially able to honor their commitment.

Every business is different, but they all require an exit strategy. Years ago, it was quite common to believe that the real advantage to being in business for yourself was that you were your own boss and didn't have to answer to anyone. Wrong!!! We all have to answer to someone: the bank, investors, spouses, etc. The only good reason to become a business owner is to generate acceptable returns. Careful planning increases the odds of your success, and exit strategies are part of that planning.

Financing Strategies

For most startup businesses, there are multiple financing sources. Does this mean that you will obtain the capital you need? Absolutely not! But you can increase the odds of success by matching likely candidates to the unique features of your business. For example, you wouldn't seek funding for a restaurant from an investor who only invests in healthcare. Nor would you seek capital for a service business from investors who want to secure their investment with business collateral. When seeking investors, here are some primary factors to consider:

- The industry
- Specific business parameters
- Geographical location
- Minority involvement
- Available collateral
- Required capital equipment
- Inventory
- Personal credit worthiness

Okay! We want to start a new business. How will we finance it? Here are some options:

Collateral-Based Bank Financing

This is the most traditional form of financing offered by banks. It means that the bank will require a business plan and will only provide a collateralized loan (generally secured by collateral familiar to the bank). The collateral will most likely be inventory, equipment, and/or real estate. The bank will take into account the liquidation value of the collateral because the business is new and at higher risk of failure. Assuming a familiarity with the inventory (having previously issued such loans), the bank will usually loan an amount equal to 50% of the cost basis. Using equipment as collateral could get you a 70% of cost loan, depending on your personal financial strength. In every case, the bank will require your, and perhaps your spouse's, personal guarantees.

The lending institution will also ask for your personal financial statement, at least three years of tax returns, your business plan and a clear understanding of how much capital you are putting into the business. In virtually all cases, the bank will want to over-collateralize the loan. It will expect you to have sufficient working capital (your investment) to sustain the business for a specific period of time. This will vary by institution. The average term of such a loan is usually no longer than five years. You should ask for several conditions. The first is to request interest-only payments for the first year. This helps to preserve cash. Second, you should ask the bank for a longer amortization period. For example, if the bank offers a five-year term, then you should see if they will give you a 7-10 year amortization with a balloon payment at the end of year five. If your business gets to that fifth year and you can't meet the balloon payment, you'll probably be able to refinance the business.

This type of loan is the least desirable way to finance your business for two reasons. First, the security agreement that the bank will require will include all assets of the business; inventory, fixtures, equipment, accounts receivable, customer lists … on and on and on! Second, the bank will probably not be willing to lend you additional money on the same collateral. This greatly reduces your ability to finance future growth during the early years of your business. Nevertheless, this may be the only way to finance some kinds of startup businesses.

If you decide to seek bank financing, be sure to visit more than one bank. When I apply for a bank loan, I always ask the banker to tell me how he can make the loan and not just reject the loan. For example, the banker may tell me that I need $50,000 more in my capital contribution to the business. At least this gives me the opportunity to go to family and friends to try to raise the $50,000, as opposed to just getting a "no" answer. Also, make sure you ask the bank to meet your timeframe with an answer. Remember, you are not there to beg. Banks make money from lending money. You want the bank to treat you as an equal, and you have every right to tell the bank your needs. If they can't meet them, go elsewhere.

There is one other condition the bank will want you to meet. They will usually insist that you maintain your operating account at the bank and may ask you to conduct your personal banking there, as well.

Finally, it's very important to know who the decision-maker is regarding your loan. Ideally, it will be the banker with whom you are dealing. But many times this is dictated by the loan amount. It may require a higher authority or even a board decision. The bad part about this is that you aren't doing the selling and therefore can't influence the decision-maker. In the section on purchasing an existing business, I will discuss the loan structure in greater detail.

Equity Investment

Many startup businesses are funded by securing outside equity investment. This is defined as providing an ownership interest in your business in exchange for the investment.

Investing in equity may take different forms, depending upon the amount of capital you will require:

1. *Individual Investor:* You may choose to raise money from a single individual investor or a small group of investors. In this case, you should make sure that these people are qualified investors. Relative to the sale of a security (either public or private), an accredited (qualified) investor is defined as an individual with over $200,000 in annual income for the past two years, an individual and spouse with combined annual income of $300,000 during the past two years, or one who has a net worth of over $1,000,000. Assuming the investment from

this individual or group is less than $500,000, you need not document this information, but you should at least verify that they are accredited.

Usually, these investors are passive investors, but not always. An active investor will want to play a role in your business, generally as a director of your company. Passive investors tend to stay out of the way. Generally, the greater the investment risk to an individual or small group, the more likely they will want frequent updates.

Proceed with caution when seeking this type of financing. Everything typically goes great in the beginning, but may not be so "hunky dory" when your business faces the almost certain glitches that will come along. Also, investors must be in this *for the long haul*. Otherwise, the investment will surely doom the new business. When creating this investment vehicle for your business, you must determine how the investor will achieve a return, and ultimately exit, from his/her investment. Without anticipating an end game, your chances of securing this investor are very unlikely.

2. *Strategic Partner:* An equity investment may come from a company interested in investing in what you are doing. We generally refer to this investor as a strategic partner. There are both negatives and positives to obtaining financing from a strategic partner. The positives usually center on both the knowledge they can provide to you and available resources (e.g., technology, services, etc.). The negatives are that once you "marry," it is likely that you won't have ultimate control of your destiny, and you can be sure that this investor will extract a huge "pound of flesh." This means that you will probably be required to give up more of your business than you would like.

   Case in point: I recently sold an information technology company in which I had a principal interest to our largest customer. Because we were squeezed between a technology partner and the customer, our selling price was far below our valuation. In many ways, this sale was forced. If we hadn't had to make this deal to survive, the outcome would have been very different.

3. *Private Placement:* On several occasions, I was very successful at raising capital from individuals in relatively small amounts, usually between $25,000 and $100,000. This involves the sale of a security and requires three legal documents: 1) a prospectus, commonly referred to as a private placement memorandum; 2) a subscription agreement governing the investment; and 3) an investor questionnaire to determine accreditation.

   The advantage to this method is that all of your investors are passive, and none is large enough to warrant inclusion on your board of directors. However, this is also a disadvantage in that once these investors put in their money, they are of no future value to your business. Other disadvantages are: 1) the legal cost involved in producing the prospectus (anywhere from $15,000 to

$50,000); 2) the time it takes before you can go to market to raise the capital; and 3) the risk of not succeeding in raising the necessary amount.

4. *Professional Venture Capital:* This is another way in which a few have the opportunity to raise capital. It's not realistic for most startup businesses because many venture capital firms: 1) invest in specific industries; 2) generally seek out businesses with either proprietary information or technology; and 3) make a limited number of investments in any given year. Nevertheless, it's worth mentioning.

   During the dot.com boom, venture capital was plentiful and available to almost anyone who had an Internet business idea. I had a $10 million commitment for the information technology company mentioned above. Unfortunately, the dot.com bust came as fast as the boom, and my $10 million went up in smoke. For the next several years, a few partners and I supported the continuation of our business, with a scaled-down product and reduced expectations. Eventually, we could not continue along this path, and entered the relationship with the two NYSE listed companies that ended up squeezing us, as I described earlier.

   Another reason I mention professional venture capital firms is that their investment philosophy is easily identified. So you don't have to waste time with those who invest in other areas. Also, if you are one of the fortunate prospects for venture capitalists, they do bring sophisticated management practices to your business and will surely have an exit plan (e.g., sale to the public via an initial public offering, sale to a corporate purchaser, etc.).

5. *Friends and Family:* Many people starting a new business raise capital from family and friends, especially when startup capital is relatively small. For some, this is very difficult. Although this is understandable, friends and family may well be the biggest source of startup capital for small business. This kind of transaction can be structured in many ways. These include straight debt, possibly secured by the assets of the business. This generally will require personal guarantees, which you will most likely want to give to your friends and family. In this case, the money is a loan, but the investor may be given a small piece of the equity as an incentive for taking the risk.

Other Loan Programs

1. *Finance/Investment Companies:* You can find these through classified ads in the *Wall Street Journal, USA Today* and *New York Times*. You also may find these firms via an Internet search. These are commonly referred to as "lenders of last resort." Many require real estate as collateral to loans that have interest rates considerably higher than bank rates. I don't recommend going to these firms, unless your business is going to sustain very high margins. Also, these companies don't generally lend to startup businesses.

2. *Inventory Financing*: In this form of financing, major suppliers will provide you with terms on your opening inventory requirements. Generally speaking, these are short-term loans, usually no longer than one year. The supplier's criteria are based on your capital investment. They may also depend on your familiarity with the industry, as well as your personal relationship with the supplier. One word of caution: Unless you know you will have sufficient capital to meet the financial terms, this type of financing can cause you nothing but headaches.

3. *Equipment Leasing*: In most cases, equipment leasing is preferable to purchasing. This is especially true in startup businesses because it preserves cash. An equipment lease usually has a buyout provision at the end of the term for as low as $1.00.

4. *Small Business Administration Loan Guaranty Program*: The SBA's primary loan guaranty program is available to startup and existing small businesses. The program provides for financing when the applicant doesn't have either sufficient internal resources or the ability to secure bank financing on its own merit. Most banks and some non-bank lenders participate in this program.

   With this scenario, the SBA approves the loan structure; the lender makes the loan; and the SBA provides a guaranty, thereby reducing the risk to the lending institution. In many cases, the lending institution actually sells the paper to entities that acquire and administer SBA guaranty loans. In order to participate in the program, the SBA looks at repayment ability from the business, character of the borrower, collateral and owner's equity contribution. However, the ratio of owner equity contribution to the loan is significantly less than that required by a bank making a conventional loan.

   Under SBA's 7(a) Loan Program, there is a $5 million limit on borrowing, and SBA's maximum exposure under its guaranty is up to 90%. Also, the terms of these loans are up to 25 years for real estate and equipment and ten years for working capital. Should there be a combination of assets and working capital, a weighted average will be used to determine the maturity date. In the past, the financing called for interest-only payments for six months, followed by monthly interest and principal payments. Interest rates are now negotiated between the borrower and the lender, but are subject to SBA maximums which are pegged to the prime rate. Interest rates may be fixed or variable. Fixed rate loans of $50,000 or more cannot exceed prime plus 2.25% if the maturity is less than seven years or prime plus 2.75% if maturity is seven years or more. On loans of less than $50,000, the interest rate allowed is greater. Variable rate loans may be pegged to either the lowest prime rate or the SBA optional peg rate. This is a weighted average of what the government pays for loans, with maturities similar to the average SBA loan. There are prepayment penalties associated with these loans.

To offset the costs of the loan program to the taxpayer, the Agency charges lenders a guaranty fee and a servicing fee, some of which can be passed on to the borrower. These are not significant enough to deter the borrower who cannot obtain capital any other way.

In seeking an SBA loan, you should find a certified lender; this will usually ensure that you will receive a decision within five business days. A certified lender can expedite the process because it is authorized to make the credit decision on behalf of the SBA.

The SBA also has a direct lending program to minorities and women. It is usually for smaller amounts. It will also fund community-sponsored lending programs designed to bring economic strength to depressed areas.

SBA plays a very important role in the growth of small business. Over the years, I have helped many clients obtain SBA loans. Depending on the ability of the business to support debt, the SBA can be a very good lending option. The SBA loan guaranty program was created to spur the growth and creation of small business. Its main advantages are: 1) it requires significantly less collateral than conventional bank financing; 2) in many cases it will accept less than a one-to-one ratio of collateral to debt; and 3) longer repayment terms.

Once your business is well established, there is another form of financing that may be available to you. This financing is the only true financing tool to finance future growth. It is called asset-based financing. The likely asset to be financed under this type is accounts receivable financing. This is where the lending institution advances payment on each invoice you submit. The business is provided a line of credit and each advance draws down the line. Each time payment from the customer is received, it is provided to the bank and credited to your line of credit. Interest is only paid as long as the invoice is outstanding. This finances growth because, as you grow, you can expand the line of credit. I will discuss this in greater detail in the next part of the course, **"How to Purchase an Existing Business"** and cite a specific program that I helped develop for the retail pharmacy industry.

This ends the section on starting a new business. I have tried to cover a broad spectrum. Each startup business has different issues that need to be addressed. I hope that you know much more than you did before reading and studying the content. Should you wish to seek additional help with any aspect of your new business venture, my firm is available to provide such assistance. Feel free to contact me at mbusch@shbconsultants.com.

Purchasing an Existing Business

Buyer Motivation

Okay! You want to buy an existing business. The first thing we have to examine is your motivation. Why do you want to buy this business? Here are some typical reasons people buy businesses:

- Looking for a better job
- Familiar with the industry
- See growth potential
- Have confidence in ability to manage
- Tired of working for others
- Seeking an equity stake
- As a customer, appreciates the business
- Consider it a family project
- Want to relocate

These are all valid reasons to buy a business – except one. Do you know which one? If you said, "Looking for a better job," you're absolutely right! Purchasing a business is an investment. That's why your motivation shouldn't be simply exchanging one salaried position for another. You have to consider how you are going to achieve an acceptable return on your monetary investment. You also need to plan how you're going to exit the business when the time comes. This should be done up front, before you complete the transaction. Although your exit strategy may change down the road, it's still important to have a plan in place.

It's essential that you honestly assess why you want this business. Otherwise, it's likely that your expectations will be unrealistic. This can make the process of operating the business more stressful than normal.

It's also important to begin to formulate your operating plan before concluding the transaction. This will not only help you to obtain financing, but will also prepare you to "hit the ground running" when you take over the business. One word of caution: Don't rush into making changes too quickly. Changes affect your customers, and unless they are carefully thought out, may adversely impact your business.

Some years ago, I bought a 2500 sq. ft. drugstore located in a very affluent community. The layout of the store was very functional except for one wall, which was completely taken up by a soda fountain. Because there was no way I could justify a third of the space being devoted to coffee drinkers, we took out the fountain and installed a very fashionable cosmetic department. Can you guess what happened? My walk-in traffic quickly dwindled to 50% of what it had been, and our home delivery business drastically increased. The problem with delivery is that it eliminates impulse buying, so our revenue dropped dramatically. Within six months, I sold the store. Had I kept it, I would have reinstalled the soda fountain … so much for making quick changes without anticipating the consequences.

Seller Motivation

Knowing why someone wants to sell their business is very important because it can give you valuable "insider" knowledge and help you in negotiation. For example, discovering that the seller is anxious about the sale can affect your offering price—or even cause you to reexamine your interest. If the seller has a great sense of urgency, you may even be able to get him to partially finance your purchase. While most of the reasons for selling a business are obvious, it's worth noting as many as we can:

- Family illness
- Seeks retirement
- Burnout
- Business downturn
- Lease considerations
- Business location issues
- Divorce
- Personnel problems
- Business upturn leading to perceived higher valuation
- Financial problems
- Other special circumstances
- Family desires relocation

It's not always easy to discover the seller's motivation. Many business owners won't be open about why they want to sell. That's why it's essential to go through the following evaluation process.

Quick-Check

This is a term that I've used for years to describe the preliminary evaluation and valuation of existing businesses. It should always be your first step in deciding whether to buy a business. Bottom line: You need to determine if the business is viable before spending a penny on legal and accounting fees.

Most businesses are sold through a "blind listing" by the seller's broker or agent. This means that the *type* of business is disclosed, but the seller is not identified. This provides two primary benefits: 1) It enables brokers to screen prospective buyers for the seller; and 2) It prevents the seller's employees and customers from learning about the sale (which could adversely affect business).

When dealing with a business broker or agent, you will probably be asked to sign a Non-Disclosure Agreement (NDA). If you are, be sure to read it carefully before signing. The NDA will most likely prohibit you from disclosing all information received about the business (except that which is public knowledge) to **anyone but those assisting you in evaluating the opportunity.** Since your evaluation team will also be bound by this agreement, they need to know you've signed an NDA. The broker may also try to determine your level of resources, but most will tread lightly in this area. Remember, he or she is usually working on a success fee and has every incentive to close the deal.

If you are dealing with a broker, he or she will probably give you a booklet or fact sheet on the seller's business, including the asking price. It will be designed to paint the best possible picture of the business, within the parameters of the financial statements. (Note: You will most likely receive a financial summary in your initial sales package, instead of actual financial statements.) After thoroughly reviewing the initial package, you should make a list of all unanswered questions. Here is a sample list of inquiries:

- *What is the gross margin?* Gross margin is generally defined as the selling price of the product/service, less any direct cost. If the business product is furniture, gross margin is the selling price less the cost of the furniture sold. What you are interested in is the percentage of gross margin.

- *What is the percentage of net profit in relationship to gross sales?* This tells you how much business you have to do in order to realize your expectations.

- *Assuming an inventory-based business, what is the average inventory on hand?* This allows you to measure inventory turn and gives you an idea of investment required to support growth. One note of caution: Inventory turn for a defined period (e.g., annual) is the *cost of sales* divided by the amount of inventory. It is not gross sales divided by inventory. Many people believe that if you do $300,000 in gross sales and your inventory is $30,000, then your average inventory turn is 10. This is an overstatement of inventory turn.

- *What are customer demographics?* This includes age range, gender, income and geographic radius of your target market.

- *Who is the competition?*

- *What are normal business hours?*

- *Describe the employees by job description and required skill set.* It is also important to know longevity of employment.

- *Request a minimum of three years of financial statements, including balance sheet, statement of profit and loss and cash flow statement.* The way in which these statements are prepared will reflect how well the business is managed.

- *Request three years of tax returns.* If the business is a C-Corporation, you'll need business returns only; if an S-Corporation or LLC, you'll need both business and personal returns; if a sole proprietorship, you'll just need personal returns.

In most cases, the answers to these questions should give you enough information to determine your level of interest—or even to prepare an offer. If the business is complex or relatively large, you'll probably need to gather additional information before making a final decision.

Letter of Intent (LOI)

After conducting your Quick-Check to confirm your interest, I recommend having an informal discussion with the seller about your offering price. If this is well received, you should then send a letter of intent (LOI). This non-binding letter is the best way to be taken seriously—and may serve as a road map to the transaction itself. In addition to pricing, the LOI may include:

- *Method of Purchase*
  Assuming the business is a corporate entity, there are two ways to complete the transaction. First, you can choose to purchase all of the tangible and intangible assets. Tangible assets are "hard assets," such as equipment, furniture and fixtures, and inventory. Intangible assets are known as "goodwill" and include such things as customer lists, market value of the business less depreciated value of hard assets, the business name, etc. I highly recommend the asset purchase method.

  The second way you can purchase the business is by buying the corporation itself. This means that you acquire all of the issued and outstanding shares of business stock. The big drawback to this method is that the buyer retains liability for anything that may have happened in the past. This is why a stock purchase requires a far more comprehensive examination. I will discuss both methods later in greater detail.

- *LOI and its purchase offer are contingent on a timely completion of a due diligence examination of the business.*

- *Timeline*
  It's very important to include a timeline in your LOI. The longer you take to complete a transaction, the greater the likelihood of additional obstacles that can impair the purchase. Adding such phrases as "We seek to complete our due diligence examination by 9-30-06; finalize terms and conditions by 10-15-06; review documents by 10-30-06 and close on or before 11-15-06" provides a definitive timeline.

- *Non-Binding Provision*
  It's very important the LOI clearly state that should you decide not to pursue the purchase, there will be no obligation to either party. (Note: Should this occur, I recommend that you return all confidential information provided by the seller.)

Remember, while you may have done some preliminary negotiation with respect to pricing, you have not closed the door on further negotiation. Until you have gone through due diligence and put your business plan together, you can't be sure that your original offer is still on the table. Conversely, just because the seller has signed off on your LOI, he or she is not bound by the offer either. In a sense, the process is like fishing. You throw out the line, and the seller bites. You may reel him in, but he can easily break the line!

But every part of the process is necessary to help you finalize the transaction to your advantage. By following my recommendations, you will: 1) Get a sense of the seller's urgency; 2) Learn how the business runs, where the deficiencies lie, and what can be done to improve profitability; and 3) Discover how much the success of the business depends upon its current owner and/or employees. Do you remember my discussion about the soda fountain in the drugstore I bought? That is an important lesson. People resist change; so generally speaking, the more cautious you are about making changes, the better.

In some cases, the buyer and seller have previous knowledge of one another, and a formal LOI is not needed. If this applies to you, by all means, bypass it and move on to the next step. You may be able to refrain from making any offer until you have completed the due diligence process. This is definitely to your advantage. However, keep in mind that just because you know the seller, you can't shortchange the due diligence process. If you and the seller are honest and cooperative, your relationship shouldn't be affected (no matter what the outcome).

Due Diligence

Before you got married, you presumably went through a dating process, spent a great deal of time together, and perhaps even lived together for a while. When you got married, you probably thought you knew everything about your spouse. This process that you went through is called "due diligence." The only difference in buying a business is that the dating period is usually much shorter. A divorce can be very costly, and making the wrong purchase decision can be just as bad—both financially and emotionally. Therefore, I want to do everything in my power to make sure that a "business divorce" is not an option for you.

Due diligence basically involves gathering as much information as you can about your prospective business. If possible, you should spend a few days observing how business is conducted. You'll be amazed at how much you will learn! You'll also need to obtain the following information:

- ***Three to Five Years of Financial Statements*** – Not only do you want to know the current condition, but you want to establish patterns. Is the business growing? Have expenses increased? Has inventory increased?

- ***Three to Five Years of Federal Income Tax Returns*** – Hopefully, the financial statements mirror the tax returns.

- ***Copies of all Supplier Agreements, Contracts and Lease Agreements*** – You need to review these to make sure that there is nothing out of the ordinary that you are assuming. You also need to make sure that all essential agreements can be assumed or transferred to new ownership. In some cases, you may have to create new agreements.

- ***Litigation*** – Is the business and/or owner a party to any pending litigation?

- ***Employee Withholding Taxes*** – Is the business current with IRS withholding deposits? You want to make sure that there are no liens on the business. You should be aware that even if a business defaults on paying employee withholding, the business owner remains liable for the actual trust fund amount. Although you have no legal responsibility for these taxes, it's important to be aware of any problems in this area.

- ***Customer Lists*** – Who are the customers? Where do they come from? What are the demographics?

- ***Aging of Accounts Receivable (A/R)*** – This is important because you will likely be purchasing the A/R and you want the purchase formula to benefit you.

- ***Payroll Records*** – What are the salaries or hourly wages of the employees?

- ***Employment Agreements*** – Do any exist? If so, what happens if the business is sold? What are the termination provisions?

- ***Employee Manual*** – Is there one? Is it thorough and up to date? If there is no manual, what are the existing work rules? Is the business in compliance with federal and state regulations?

- **Employee Benefits** – What are the benefits? What are the business' contributory costs? Who is entitled to benefits?

- **Creditor Lists** – Who are the company's suppliers? Are there any secured creditors, and if so, what is the security that is pledged? *If and when you purchase the business, you want all assets to be free and clear when they are transferred to you.*

- **UCC Search** – Your attorney should do a UCC search to determine if any liens against the assets have been filed.

- **Gross Profit** – This is the difference between the selling price of goods or services and the direct cost of the goods or services. For example, a table sells for $100 and costs $50. The gross profit is $50 and the gross margin is 50%. If the business is guided by markup instead of gross margin, the markup in this case is 100%. If the table sells for $100 and costs $60, the gross profit is $40, the gross margin is 40% and the markup is 60%.

- **Inventory Turns** – If you're buying an inventory-based business, you need to know what the normal inventory turn is for the industry. You'll also want to know the annual inventory turn for the specific business. You can determine this by obtaining the inventory level at cost and dividing it by the cost of the goods sold for the entire year. For example let's assume that your inventory is $50,000, your annual sales are $1,000,000, and your gross margin for the year is 40%. Therefore, your cost of goods is 60% of the $1,000,000 or $600,000. $600,000 divided by $50,000 = 12 inventory turns for the year. Inventory turn is a strong indicator of how much money you will need to manage and grow your business. If the current owner isn't turning enough inventory, you may be able to improve the turns through better inventory management.

- **Key Employees** – Who is key to the success of the business? Are you going to be able to retain those key employees?

- **Purchasing Methods** – Find out as much as you can about how goods are purchased. Who are the primary suppliers? What are typical payment terms?

- **Systems and Procedures** – Get as much information as possible about the administration of the business. Is it computerized? If so, what operating system does it use? Is the business networked? Does it require special software?

- **Technical Aspects** – Are there any unusual technical aspects to the business?

- **Location** – Are there any planned changes that could affect business (e.g., a new road that would affect traffic or nearby building renovation)?

- **Competition** – Who is your competition? A competitor next door (especially a national or regional chain) is good for business because it draws more people to your location. A competitor two blocks away could have a neutral or negative effect.

If the seller doesn't have all the items you request, be sure you have enough information to determine if you can hold the business together—and make reasonable projections for growth.

Pricing

We've already established that the seller provided an asking price and that your LOI (Letter of Intent) included a tentative purchase price for the business. It's very important that you do your homework before deciding on the final price that you're willing to pay. Here are some key points to keep in mind:

1. Ask the seller to tell you how he arrived at the asking price.
2. Find out the industry norms for various purchase formulas.
3. Keep in mind that seller financing may impact the purchase price.

Depending upon the industry, here are the most common generic formulas used in establishing a purchase price:

- X times annual gross revenue
- X times EBITDA (earnings before interest, taxes, depreciation and amortization)
- Inventory plus one year EBITDA (in some cases more than one year EBITDA)
- Any of the above plus an "earn out" (defined as a percentage of the profits over some period of time)

No matter which purchase formula is used, the critical element in establishing a price is the payback period. If the total purchase price is recovered in three or less years, you have a very good deal. If it takes longer than five years, you've probably paid too much for the business. I typically try to recover my investment in three to four years.

Negotiation

Generally speaking, I find that negotiation has more to do with terms and conditions of purchase rather than the purchase price. Sometimes the purchase price has to be tweaked to satisfy certain situations affecting the seller. If you as the purchaser base your offer on the payback period, then there won't be a lot of room for you to negotiate the price. However, there are some trade-offs that occur in negotiations. As a rule of thumb, if you offer some concession in pricing or in terms, then you should get something in return. Depending on the complexity of the transaction, you might want an intermediary to negotiate on your behalf. The advantage to this for both sellers and buyers is that the intermediary can't make the final decision and can't get trapped. There were many times when my representatives brought back a demand from the other side. In a number of these situations, I delayed making a decision, and the other side backed off. In these cases, the other side wanted the transaction badly, and I was able to tell just how far I could push.

A word of caution: Most of the time, deals get done because they are win/win for the parties. You need to be very careful in the selection of your attorney. I always try to choose a lawyer who wants to make—and not break—the deal. The latter will never serve you well. Furthermore, your counsel should not be there to make business decisions. He or she needs to simply point out the legal risks and tell you the best way to overcome them. Transactions can only occur with some compromising on both sides. And while it's very important to be protected by proper agreements, the truth of the matter is that contracts are only as good as the parties who sign them. Otherwise, all you have is litigation—and only the lawyers win.

Terms and Conditions of Purchase

As a practical matter, when you buy a business, it will most likely be an asset purchase. This means you are buying all the assets of the business and assuming no liabilities. So let's define the assets that you might be buying:

- *Tangible Assets* - Includes inventory, equipment, furniture and fixtures, and real estate.

- *Intangible Assets* - Includes customer lists, trademarks, trade names, telephone numbers, and agreements that you wish to assume.

- *Accounts Receivable* - This is a tangible asset, but it should be handled differently. In order to ensure the continuity of the business, it's in your best interest to collect the accounts receivable for the seller. One way to handle this is to buy them under a formula (e.g., 50% cash and the balance in 90 days, after which any uncollected A/R goes back to the seller). The other method is to collect the A/R for the seller and give him the proceeds at the end of each 30-day period. Again, after 90 days, the uncollected accounts are returned to seller.

- *Goodwill* - Goodwill is the difference between your purchase price and the book value of the tangible assets.

Let's briefly discuss how an asset purchase is structured. There are tax ramifications for the parties relative to the purchase of goodwill. I'm not an accountant, so I won't give tax advice. However, because goodwill is taxable to the seller, he or she will want to do everything possible to minimize tax consequences. Conversely, goodwill is amortized by the buyer, resulting in a reduction in assets on the balance sheet each year. One way to reduce goodwill is to provide the seller with a "Covenant Not to Compete Agreement" as part of the transaction. Your accountant can advise on how much of the purchase price can be attributed to the non-compete, and on the related tax ramifications.

Required Documentation

The most important document is the Asset Sale and Purchase Agreement. This spells out exactly what you are purchasing, the terms and conditions under which you are buying the business, and monetary consideration. The agreement will also specify terms of the seller's non-compete provisions, warranties and indemnification clauses and will contain various schedules that the seller will be required to prepare. The schedules that your attorney will require are directly dependent on the nature and complexity of the business. Here is a list of some of the more common schedules that will be part of the Asset Sale and Purchase Agreement.

- *Inventory Valuation* - This schedule will describe in detail how the inventory being purchased is valued. Inventory can be categorized in several ways: 1) good inventory usually purchased at cost, 2) obsolete inventory that may be purchased at a discount, and 3) outdated inventory that will not be purchased. There are generally industry standards as to how inventory is valued.

- *Litigation* - The seller must attest to or deny any pending or anticipated litigation.*Tangible Assets* - This is a comprehensive list of all assets being sold.

- *IP Assets Software Licenses* - If there are IP assets and software licenses, they would be listed on this schedule. It's also important that the seller arrange for the transfer of these licenses.

- *Foreign Jurisdictions* - A list of states and/or countries where the business has filed an application to do business.*Title to Assets* - Seller represents that he or she has title to the assets being sold and is authorized to sell them. This is also where the seller would identify any creditor that has a security interest in the assets (e.g., a bank or supplier).

- *Taxes* - Seller is required to provide a statement regarding any tax deficiency or delinquency. If none, the seller must provide a warranty that the business is in compliance with all taxing authorities.

- *Marks* - Seller will list any trademarks, trade names or patents registered to the business.

- *Contracts* - Seller will provide a comprehensive list of all active contracts, including lease agreements and employment contracts.

- *Environmental Issues* - This schedule is required to protect the buyer.

- *Insurance* - A list of all insurance coverage along with the policies.

- *Employee Benefits* - Seller lists all employee benefits currently provided.

- *Financial Statements* - The financial statements that you previously reviewed should be added to the agreement. You may also want your accountant to review the statements.

The Asset Sales and Purchase Agreement should contain all representations made to you by the seller, especially those that were material to your purchase decision. This Agreement is designed to protect you in the event that the seller made material misrepresentations.

Additional agreements may include the building lease (either assigned to you or an executed new lease); equipment leases, software licenses, and assigned contracts. This is an area that a buyer can easily overlook.Your attorney may also require a separate Covenant Not to Compete Agreement, as well as other agreements that may apply.

Personnel Retention

During due diligence, it is important that you ask the seller to provide an honest assessment of his personnel. If at all possible, don't make any sudden changes to your employees or the basic business operation. As established earlier, change in fundamentals that is not well thought out can really have a negative impact on the business.

If they don't already exist, you'll need to create job descriptions for all employees. Written job descriptions will enable you to better evaluate existing personnel. They will also help you to hire according to the job description. One of the great mistakes in business is hiring because you like someone, then being forced to build the job around them.

As the owner of the business, you have a great responsibility and obligation when it comes to hiring. If you hire the wrong person, it's your fault. It will also impact your other employees. If you hire wrong, try to correct it as soon as possible. Make sure you have a copy of the employee manual. If none, be prepared to write a manual.

The Business Plan

In the section on **"Starting a New Business,"** we spent a good deal of time talking about your business plan. But planning for an existing business requires a slightly different mindset. First of all, this plan must be based upon data from past operations. Second, it is likely that you will use it to obtain financing for both the purchase and any additional working capital that might be needed.

I suggest using the same format as that previously discussed. However, your approach needs to be different, and the headings in the table of contents will change slightly.

Executive Summary

I would start off by identifying the business, its location, its products and its ownership. Here is an example:

Introduction
Pursuant to a Letter of Intent dated March 1, 2006, I, John Davis intend to purchase G.H. Reilly Furniture Co. located at 130 Avalon Street in Naperville, Illinois. The store specializes in middle market living room and family room furnishings, bedroom, dining room and patio furniture along with compatible accessories featuring the designs of ABC, DEF and XYZ (see products). The Company was founded by George Reilly in 1989 and has been a fixture in Naperville since that time. The business occupies 10,000 square feet of leased premises, of which 8,000 square feet is devoted to showroom selling space and the balance for office and warehousing.

Naperville is the fourth largest city in Illinois and has been the state's fastest growing community. As the community has grown, so has G.H. Reilly. The business has experienced growth every year since its inception. Mr. Reilly has been very active in local affairs and I expect to continue that trend. Further, Mr. Reilly has agreed to stay on as a consultant for a period of six months and will be available on an "as needed" basis.

2005 gross revenue was $1.2 million with an EBITDA of $300,000. 1ˢᵗ Quarter revenue was up 8.3% over the same period of 2005.

At this point, I suggest getting right to what financing you are seeking, the purchase price and the security behind the loan. In the example below you'll notice that I suggest securing the loan with the business assets. I make no mention of personal guaranty, but it's quite likely that you, and perhaps your wife, will have to provide a personal guaranty.

The Acquisition
The transaction, an asset sale/purchase, is expected to be completed by June 30. The purchase price is $840,000 or 3.5 times EBITDA. The acquirer is seeking financing in the amount of $640,000 to be secured by the assets of the business (see Balance Sheet as of 3-30-06).

Operating History
The following represents the five-year performance of G.H. Reilly Furniture Co.

	In (000s)				
	2001	2002	2003	2004	2005
Revenue	$750	900	980	1.058	1.2
EBITDA	$172	225	245	265	300

(See Accompanying Financial Statements)

G.H. Reilly Furniture Co. is a Sub-chapter S-Corporation. The acquirer also intends to form a Sub-S Corporation as the legal structure for operating the business. Allocating 35% to taxes, a $50,000 draw to support borrower's cost of living and assuming <u>no growth</u>, the loan will be retired in less than five years.

In the example above, it is assumed that the buyer invested $200,000 of his/her own money. The buyer should check with an accountant to see how much of this $200,000 can be structured as a loan to the Sub-S Corporation, which may be paid back without tax consequence.

Products
In this section you should describe the product selection, provide vendor information, terms and conditions of product purchases (e.g., 30 days net), and highlight the price-point range. Here is an example:

The company offers a complete line of upholstered living room and family room furniture, cocktail and end tables, casual chairs, bedroom and dining room furniture along with compatible accessories. Its vendors are A, B, C, D, E, and F. Normal terms in the industry are 30 days net, and in the case of some vendors, terms extend to 60 days net. The price points range from a low of $195 for some tables to a high of $1,795 for sofas. Chairs range in price from $295 to $795. However, approximately 55% of sales are catalog sales, which reduces inventory carrying costs.

Competition
Be sure to fully describe your competition. Competition is a good thing. Show me a business that has no competition, and you'll probably show me one that doesn't have a ready market. Most businesses benefit from good competition and suffer from bad. Inferior competitors reflect poorly on your business and can even cause potential customers to look outside your immediate area. And don't forget the Internet as a competitor. Nevertheless, you can position competitors to your advantage. Look at the following:

There are three competitors, Armstrong Furniture, Davis Interiors and Wallace Furniture serving the same market. Two of the three, Armstrong and Davis are located within one and one-half blocks of G.H. Reilly. This actually benefits

G.H. Reilly because the three stores share the same traffic. A customer going to one of the stores is likely to visit all three. Wallace Furniture is located at one end of the town on Highway 24.

There is a Costco super-store located just outside Naperville. Costco occasionally offers furniture specials, but selection is very limited. Costco does offer quality products and low prices. However, because of its limited and varying product selection, it is not considered a direct competitor.

The Internet must also be considered a competitor. Most any item carried in the store can be obtained over the Internet. Pricing in general is consistent with that being offered from the retail store, but there are times when items are priced lower. The one disadvantage to purchasing furniture over the Internet is that a large percentage of furniture arrives damaged. Unless the Internet store has a local arrangement regarding repair, it is at a significant disadvantage. Further, those that do have such an arrangement are more likely to be priced at conventional retail.

All of the above are worthy competitors and must be taken seriously. In the past G.H. Reilly has marketed well enough to sustain substantial growth year after year.

The Market

There are three things that <u>must</u> appear in this section: 1) description of target audience; 2) market size; and 3) traffic count (both driving and walking, if available). Here's how I would state this information:

G. H. Reilly targets an age group of 30-55. Its furniture is more contemporary than traditional and its price-points favor this target audience. Purchase patterns are consistent with other furniture retailers in that women account for approximately 70% of purchase decisions. Even in cases where wives bring their husbands, the decision is generally left to the woman. Therefore, on-the-floor merchandising is geared toward attracting the female shopper.

Naperville has a population of 125,000 and a metropolitan trading area of 200,000 people. 65% of the trading area consists of households with an average of two children and an adult population within the target audience.

The city's department of transportation estimates that 8,500 automobiles drive the 100 block of Avalon Street within a 24-hour period. Because the store is located in the middle of Naperville's downtown shopping district, there is also significant walk-by traffic. The area houses an abundance of retail shops, restaurants and offices. Parking is readily available in a nearby garage and is free to G.H. Reilly patrons.

Marketing Plan

This is where you have to lay out your plan—not just what Reilly has done in the past. Remember that your financial plan has to show growth; otherwise, why buy the business? And it's the marketing plan that's going to produce that growth.

Depending upon the industry, there are various elements that make up the marketing plan. In the case of this furniture store, I would approach the marketing plan like this:

Advertising
G.H. Reilly has consistently placed weekly ads in the Naperville newspaper. We plan to continue this practice and are in the process of reviewing all previous ads to determine which were the most effective. This will also help determine our business cycle.

Direct Mail/Email
We expect to budget for a monthly direct mail campaign to existing customers as well as our target market. We will also send monthly email ads and special sale notices to our current customers via email.

Newsletter
We intend to develop a G.H. Reilly newsletter to showcase our customers and their children. It will highlight their contributions to the community, including excellence in sports, public service, charitable giving, etc. We will also provide gift certificates for outstanding achievement. People love to see their names in print, so the newsletter will be designed to present our customers in the best light possible. It will also include information on new products as they are launched.

In-store
Because 70% of the purchase decisions are made by women, we will display our furniture with this in mind. We will also place silk flower arrangements throughout the store, to keep the display floor bright, cheerful and airy.

Typically, furniture is always bought on sale. Although the markup is 100%, sale prices reduce margin. We intend to test a concept that I call "magic pricing." Magic pricing differs from the usual "we are having a sale" method. When we magic-price an item, that price will continue as long as there is demand for the item. Only when there is no longer a demand will we raise the price back to normal markup.

The theory behind this is if I normally sell a table for $299 and it costs $150, I can lower the price as long as I sell more. For example, if I sell one table a month at $299, I make a gross profit of $149. But if I sell two tables a month at $249 each, I make a gross profit of $198. Therefore, I can afford to keep the magic price for as long as there is demand. As soon as demand stops, the price is raised.

This differs from most retailers who take items that do not move and put them on sale. The problem is that without demand for the item, you're not likely to move many, even at the sale price.

We also intend to expand the store's line of accessories. While many of these additional items will be used to enhance furniture displays, each will be available for sale. Suggestive selling of a displayed bowl with a cocktail table can increase both sales and margin. The same will apply to artwork displayed on the walls above the furniture.

We believe that adherence to this total marketing effort will stimulate sales growth consistent with the pro forma provided in the business plan.

Management

This is where you spotlight your experience in the workplace. If you're experienced in the industry, then you can take a straightforward approach. If you don't have direct industry experience, then you need to clearly show how your abilities qualify you to successfully operate this business. Because they try to avoid risk, most banks put a lot of emphasis on the borrower's skillset.

In addition to describing your own background, you should include that of key employees. In the case of this furniture store, you could also list Mr. O'Reilly as a consultant and describe his qualifications.

One of the major reasons businesses fail is because the right individuals are not in the right jobs. It's worth repeating, **financing sources put a lot of stock in the perceived strength of management.**

Financial Plan

This is the "make or break" section of your business plan. I can't emphasize enough the importance of checking the numbers over and over for errors. They *must* be correct! This may sound obvious, but simple mistakes can cost you valuable credibility with bankers and potential investors.

This section should contain the financial statements provided by the business owner. Ideally, you should include at least three years of comprehensive statements. This includes balance sheet, P & L and cash flow statements. It's also a good idea to attach a brief explanation to each year's statement explaining any unusual activity that impacted financial performance (e.g., a growth curve or revenue drop).

After the financial statements, you should include three years of future growth projections. These should reflect the expected results of additional marketing, merchandise expansion, etc. Remember, your projections should always be prepared monthly and consolidated at the end of each year.

As stated earlier, an Excel spreadsheet is the best way to present your projections.

Also, while you may not be able to show enough detail in the current owner's financial statements, the more detail you can add in the projections, the better.

Next, you should add the assumptions. Using the furniture store as our business, here are some sample assumptions:

Revenue Assumptions
- Gross Margin – Margin on furniture items is calculated at 40%. Although most furniture is marked up 100% or more, the 40% margin shows the impact of discounted sale prices. Margin on accessories is 50%.

- Revenue Categories – Furniture sales account for 90% of revenue, and accessories are 10% of total. Furniture categories are bedroom, dining room, living room, patio and casual furniture.

Cost Assumptions
- Variable Expenses – Sales commissions = 5% on all items, excluding those on sale.

The assumptions would typically be placed before the pro forma financials. Because these are so brief, I would simply footnote them on the Excel P&L.

The next six pages provide formatting examples of a balance sheet, profit and loss statement, and cash flow statements. In the Exhibits section, you'll also find a complete business plan that I created for a dot.com venture. Because this plan was for a very complex business seeking $10 million in funding, its financial plan was quite extensive. Your business will probably not require this amount of detail, but I thought it would be helpful to have an actual plan to guide you.

Balance Sheet (Projected)

Enter your Company Name here

	Beginning as of mm/dd/yyyy		Projected as of mm/dd/yyyy

Assets

Current Assets

Cash in bank	$		$
Accounts receivable Inventory Prepaid expenses			
Other current assets	_____	-	_____ -
Total Current Assets	$	-	$

Fixed Assets

Machinery & equipment	$		$
Furniture & fixtures			
Leasehold improvements			
Land & buildings			
Other fixed assets			
(LESS accumulated depreciation on all fixed assets)	_____	-	_
Total Fixed Assets (net of depreciation)	$_____	-	$

Other Assets

Intangibles	$		$
Deposits			
Goodwill			
Other	_____	-	_
Total Other Assets	$	-	$
TOTAL Assets Liabilities and Equity			

Current Liabilities

Accounts payable
Interest payable
Taxes payable
Notes, short-term (due within 12 months)
Current part, long-term debt
Other current liabilities
Total Current Liabilities

Long-term Debt

Bank loans **payable** Notes payable to stockholders
LESS: Short-term portion
            Other long term debt
            Total Long-term Debt

Total Liabilities

Owners' Equity

Invested capital
Retained earnings - beginning
Retained earnings - current
Total Owners' Equity

Total Liabilities & Equity

[Your Company Name]
Income Statement for Year Ending
mm/dd/yrl

Revenue
        Gross Sales
        Less Returns & Allowances   _____
        Net Sales

Cost of Goods Sold
        Beginning Inventory
Add: Purchases
        Freight In
        Direct Labor

Less: Ending Inventory

Cost of Goods Sold   _____

Gross Profit (Loss)

Expenses
        Advertising
        Charitable Contributions
        Maintenance & Repairs
        Telephone
        Utilities
        Supplies
        Rent
        Depreciation/Amortization
        Bank Charges
        Contract Labor
        Postage and Printing
        Officer Salaries
        Payroll Taxes & Benefits
        Wages
        Payroll Taxes & Benefits
        Property Taxes
        Vehicle & Delivery Expense
        Travel
        Interest Expense   _____

Net Operating Income

Other Income   _____

Net Income

[Your Company Name]
Income Statement For the Year
Ended [Mmmm Dd, 200X]

Net Operating Income		**$0.00**
Other Income:		
Gain (Loss) on Sale of Assets	$0.00	
Interest Income	$0.00	
Total Other Income		**$0.00**
Net Income (Loss)		**$0.00**

THE CASH FLOW STATEMENT

The Cash Flow Statement is the most critical planning tool for a new or growing business. It shows how much cash will be needed, when it will be needed and where it will come from. It attempts to budget monthly cash needs, and shows the flow of cash into the business from sales, collection of receivables; and out of the business through payment of expenses and loans over a period of time. The banker uses this information to analyze possible shortfalls of cash and as a guide to borrowing needs. Thus, business and bank are planning together. Your statement should show Cash Flow over the full twelve-month period. This Cash Flow Statement (reprinted from SBA *Management Aid 1.001 the* ABC's *of Borrowing*) represents *a.* cash flow statement for a three month period.

CASH BUDGET
(For three months, ending March 31)

	January	February	March
	Budget	Budget	Budget
	Actual	Actual	Actual

SEE NEXT PAGE

By combining the monthly cash flow reports with an income statement for the year and your beginning and ending balance sheet, you will produce a statement of annual cash flow from operations. The monthly cash flow statement shows your need for seasonal borrowing, while the annual cash flow from operations shows the need for longer-term funds.

Expected Cash Receipts						
1. Cash sales						
2. Collections on accounts receivable						
3. Other income						
4. Total cash receipts						

Expected Cash Payments

5. Raw materials						
6. Payroll						
7. Other factory expenses (including maintenance)						
8. Advertising						
9. Selling expense						
10. Administrative expense (including salary of owner -manager)						
11. New plant and equipment						
12. Other payments (taxes, including estimated income tax; repayment of loans; interest; etc.)						
13. Total cash payments						
14. Expected cash balance at beginning of the month						
15. Cash increase or decrease (item 4 minus item 13)						
16. Expected cash balance at end of month (item 14 plus item 15)						
17. Desired working cash balance						
18. Short-term loans needed (item 17 minus item 16, if item 17 is larger)						
19. Cash available for dividends, capital cash expenditures, and/or short investments (item 16 minus item 17, if item 16 is larger than item 17)						

Capital Cash

20. Cash available (item 19 after deducting dividends etc.)						
21. Desired capital cash (item 11, new plant equipment)						
22. Long-term loans needed (item 21 less 20, if item 21 is larger than item 20)						

BE the BOSS

BE THE
BOSS

_____

_____

_____

_____

_____

_____

_____

_____

_____

_____

_____

_____

_____

_____

_____

_____

_____

_____

BE THE BOSS

_____

_____

_____

_____

_____

_____

_____

_____

_____

_____

_____

_____

_____

_____

_____

_____

_____

_____

_____

_____

_____

_____

_____

_____

BE THE BOSS

_____

_____

_____

_____

_____

_____

_____

_____

_____

_____

_____

_____

_____

_____

_____

_____

_____

_____

_____

_____

_____

_____

_____

_____

BE THE BOSS

_____

_____

_____

_____

_____

_____

_____

BE
THE
BOSS

_____

_____

_____

_____

_____

_____

BE THE BOSS

BE THE BOSS

Financing

In the "Starting a New Business" section, I spent a great deal of time on the various ways to finance your business. In this section, I'm going to concentrate only on those that are most commonly used when buying a small business. You must first be sure that your financing goals are realistic. For example, if you have $50,000 to invest and the business you want to buy has a price tag of $1 million, it's highly unlikely that you'll be able to secure sufficient financing.

As a general rule, you'll need to invest approximately 30% of the purchase price to obtain conventional bank financing. You'll also need to have a good credit history. Most important, you must be able to convince the bank that you have the skills and work ethic to effectively manage the business. When seeking bank financing, I would ask for one year of interest-only payments, a five-year term, and a seven-year amortization. Will you get those terms? It's anybody's guess, but at least it's a good starting point. I certainly wouldn't accept a loan with less than a five-year term. As stated earlier, I always aim for a payback period of three to four years.

If you can't meet the 30% threshold, you may be able to get additional financing from family and friends. However, they'll have to understand that they'll be behind the bank in terms of a secured position, and that the loan is long term.

You can also obtain additional capital by selling equity in the business. But this should be a last resort. If at all possible, I strongly recommend refraining from having investor-partners. The only positive thing an investor typically gives you is capital. And the wrong investor can actually damage your ability to control your destiny. In short, if this is your first adventure in entrepreneurship, you certainly don't need the added headache of investors!

You may also want to consider the Small Business Association (SBA) guaranteed loan program. This type of loan comes from a bank or other commercial lender and is guaranteed up to 80% by the SBA. This actually reduces the lender's risk. There are several distinct advantages to going this route: 1) The loan term is longer than conventional financing (usually seven years, and in some cases, as long as ten years); 2) The ratio of your invested capital to the loan amount is generally less than the 30% threshold mentioned above; and 3) The application process gives you more time to build a relationship with the lender. At the back of this guide, you'll find an SBA application and some helpful pamphlets.

Perhaps the best way to obtain financing is through the seller. One of the reasons I like seller financing is because it tells me that the seller has faith in the business. Unfortunately, this form of financing is not always available. But when it is, I urge you to seriously consider it.

One final note about supplier financing. Although it may sound appealing, I don't recommend it because: 1) It's usually available as short-term only, and 2) It limits your flexibility in purchasing decisions because of obligation to the supplier. You may, however, want to take advantage of equipment leasing.

No matter how you finance your business, make sure you have an accountant, attorney, or qualified consultant review all documents before they are submitted. This will help ensure your compliance with all loan covenants.

Closing the Transaction

Due diligence has been completed, your purchase price has been accepted, the various purchase and lease documents have been executed and financing is in place. It is time to close the transaction. I strongly recommend that you schedule your closing date on the last day of the month to limit the amount of pro-rated fees. No matter what industry you're in, a comprehensive inventory must be taken on the day of closing, per the Asset Purchase/Sale Agreement. Inventory should be taken by a mutually acceptable third party. Once inventory is completed, there may be some adjustments to the purchase price. This is why you should reserve some of the purchase price (in escrow with your attorney) until the adjusted amount is determined.

Buying a Franchise

Introduction & Introspection

Before we begin to discuss who should buy a franchise, let's talk about what makes a good franchise. The franchisee/franchisor relationship is pretty much like a marriage. The perceived value is at its highest the day you get married … or the day you sign the franchise agreement. Sure, nervousness kicks in, but you've made the decision to go forward and you look forward to the benefits. Like marriage, franchising is all about trying to maintain that perceived value. Sometimes it works, and sometimes it doesn't.

If we stop to examine the franchises that offer the best value proposition, one quality stands out among all others: **name recognition**! A franchise should have enough name recognition that the franchisee couldn't afford to take the sign down, even if allowed. The franchise that proves this premise best is McDonald's. Not only do they continue to generate recognition; they also offer an excellent operating system. But it's name recognition that feeds its value proposition. Customers go to McDonald's because of recognition. They don't go because it's Michael Busch's franchise.

On the other hand, a franchise without recognition must work even harder to sustain its value proposition. Once you learn the system and gain loyal customers through your own efforts, you begin to question the value of the franchising fees you are paying. As you can see, franchising can easily become a *"What have you done for me, lately"* business.

That's why franchising only works if both the franchisor and franchisee are on the same page. A good franchisee candidate must:

- Be able to adapt to a business system and not deviate too far from it.
- Recognize the need to be a team player.
- Be open to learning from others, including more successful franchisees.
- Have a positive and focused attitude.
- Be able to successfully communicate with customers and employees.
- Be willing to risk investment dollars—with someone else calling most of the shots.
- Recognize the value proposition and then make a long-term commitment to it. Believe in the franchisor's continued ability to contribute to his/her success.

- Not be overly experienced in the business. It's a misconception that the franchisor wants you to know the business. You'll actually have to unlearn some of your skills in order to succeed in this environment.
- Have a strong work ethic and be willing to put in long hours to get the business up and running.
- Share common values with the franchisor. This will create a much smoother relationship.

I can't emphasize enough the value of introspection in deciding to buy a franchise. If you're not honest in assessing your qualifications up front, you could make a very serious economic mistake.

By the way, if you decide that you are not a good candidate for a franchise, so be it. It doesn't in any way diminish your attributes or ability to succeed in an entrepreneurial environment. I'm sure that I was much better at being a franchisor (of Medicine Shoppe) than I would have been as a franchisee.

Finding the Right Franchise

The number of franchise offerings is virtually endless. This is because franchising enables a business model to be expanded at a much faster rate than privately/independently-owned units, since the franchisee is co-investing in the business expansion. So how should you look for the right franchise?

If possible, start by attending an International Franchise Association trade show. You can skip this step if you already have selected an industry to explore. However, I strongly encourage attendance because it's such an excellent learning experience.

Next, you should determine what size investment you would be most comfortable with, including both cash and debt.

Then ask yourself the following questions:

- Does the business model appear to be something that can be successfully cloned?
- Is it likely that you can recover your investment within three to five years (after taking a realistic salary)?
- Can you accept the time requirements for running the business?
- Do you have the skillset to be able to successfully manage the business?
- Are you passionate about the business model?
- Is your family excited about the opportunity?
- Do you meet the qualifications to become a franchisee?
- Can you envision operating this business for the next five to ten years?

These are just a few of the preliminary questions you should ask yourself. Some can be answered immediately; others will need to be addressed after you decide to pursue the opportunity and complete due diligence. When you answer these questions, you need to be totally honest with yourself. Remember, the next step is to get engaged — then you have to determine whether you want to get married.

Due Diligence

Uniform Franchise Offering Circular

The first step in gathering franchise information is requesting an information package (by phone or via the franchisor's website). This typically consists of a promotional brochure and qualification form.

Each franchisor is also legally required to publish a full disclosure statement, known as the Uniform Franchise Offering Circular (UFOC). This comprehensive document covers every aspect of franchise operations, including costs, restrictions, territory, training, and in some cases, earnings projections. It also includes audited financial statements. Because the UFOC is critically important in determining if a franchise is right for you, **be sure that you read it carefully, from cover to cover**.

By law, all franchisors must send the UFOC to prospective franchisees before their first personal meeting or at least ten days before payment of the initial franchise fee—whichever comes first. Because this information is in the public domain, you do *not* have to qualify to receive it. Since it is indispensable to the due diligence process, I strongly recommend that you ask for it when you request your information package.

For a complete overview of the UFOC, please see the "Regulations & Requirements" section or visit www.franchise.org.

Corporate Headquarters Visit

Once you've confirmed a serious interest in the franchise—and the company has expressed interest in you—you're ready to arrange a visit to the franchise headquarters. Although some franchisors will share in the cost of this visit, most will expect you to cover it. Your willingness to do this shows them that you are a serious candidate. Additional requirements for a corporate visit will vary. Some companies may require a refundable deposit along with the qualification form, while others may require a Letter of Intent. There is no set policy. Just make sure you receive good legal advice before sending an LOI and/or making a refundable deposit.

Each company will also conduct its prospective franchisee visits differently. To save time and money, some may invite several candidates to attend "opportunity days." Others may schedule individual sessions. In any event, this is where you have a firsthand opportunity to meet the "players," those to whom you may tie your business future. It's crucial to remember that your visit is essentially a sales opportunity for the franchisor; they want to put their very best foot forward. On the other hand, you want to get as much "behind the scenes" information as you can. So keep your eyes and ears open.

To give you a taste of what to expect, I want to share how we conducted the process at Medicine Shoppe International (MSI). After approving their qualification form, we invited the franchisee and his/her spouse to come to our corporate headquarters in St. Louis. A franchise sales consultant would meet them at the airport (or their hotel), take them on a tour of local stores, and then bring them to our offices. In the early stages of MSI franchising, I would personally take them on a tour of the building, placing great emphasis on our training center. This was MSI's answer to McDonald's University in suburban Chicago. Then I spent the rest of the day presenting the program. But here's the important part: During the morning session, I would talk about **if they purchased a franchise.** At lunch I would talk about **when they bought a franchise.** Around 2:00 PM, I would talk about **their franchise.** And at 4:00 PM, I would ask them **why I should sell them a franchise.** In essence, I was dangling the carrot and then pulling it back. I built up their excitement and then made them convince me that they were worthy candidates.

To some extent, your franchisor visit will probably be similar to this process. It's helpful to be aware of this, so you won't be unduly influenced by this interviewing technique.

You should also know that most franchisors consider this a *mutual* interview. Choosing the right franchisee is just as important to them as it is to you!

During your visit to corporate headquarters, you should try to meet as many people in operations as possible—especially those you would be working with in the future. You should also observe how they interact with each other. Personalities play a big part in every business relationship. This is even truer of the franchisor/franchisee partnership.

During your corporate visit, be sure to check out the franchisor's training program. Is it conducted at corporate headquarters or at your location? How much training is provided? Does it include detailed startup information, marketing direction and support, operational assistance, etc.?

Do your homework before making this visit and think of it as a "fact-finding mission." Read the UFOC very carefully, study the financial statements, and list as many questions as possible. When you make your visit, you can then compare what you see with what you read. Be sure you ask management about any past and pending litigation. Although some litigation is normal for franchise companies, a high number of claims could be a "red flag" that they haven't lived up to their agreements.

Finally, take visual stock of the company. Does it present a successful image? Pay attention to your instincts and don't leave without getting satisfactory answers to all of your questions. Remember, this is your best chance to determine if this franchise is right for you!

Franchisee Visits

Contacting franchisees, both in person and by telephone, is perhaps the most valuable part of the information-gathering process. The UFOC will typically contain a list of current franchise owners and those who have left the company within the past year. Some franchisors may also give you a separate list of selected franchisees. To give you an unbiased perspective on franchise ownership, it's critically important to assemble your own contact list. The best place to start is by confirming that the UFOC list contains contact information for all current franchisees. You should also request names and addresses of any who have left (voluntarily or involuntarily) within the past three years. Prospective franchisees are legally entitled to receive this information in every state.

The total number of active franchises should determine how many to contact. For example, if the company is new at franchising and has less than 150 franchises, I recommend you contact at least 20% of the stores (but no fewer than 15 franchisees). On the other hand, if it's a much larger franchise company, you should contact a smaller percentage of franchisees. For example, a company with 1,000 franchises would warrant a 2.5% contact rate, or 25 franchisees (a workable maximum, for most people). You should also try to contact as many inactive franchisees as possible. When talking to those who left involuntarily, remember that there are "two sides to every story." But their input is indispensable in gaining a balanced view.

When you assemble your contact list, divide it into two categories: on-site visits and telephone interviews. While you'll probably be able to visit only a few nearby franchisees, you should plan to call several in other geographic areas. When scheduling either personal or telephone interviews, be sure to call the franchisee several days in advance to request an appointment at their convenience.

You should have an extensive list of questions for both on-site and telephone interviews. These should include:

- When did you start the business?
- How long did it take you to open after you executed the franchise agreement?
- Are you profitable and if so, how long did it take to reach profitability?
- Is there any seasonality to the business?
- Did the franchise meet your expectations? Any surprises?
- How do you rate franchisor support?
- Did the training meet your expectations?
- What experience did you have in this industry?
- How would you compare your franchise to the financial and business models described in the UFOC?
- How many hours are you devoting to the business?
- Who is your competition?
- What are the keys to building the business?
- Have you had any personnel issues?
- What lessons have you learned that will make my entry easier?

If possible, I suggest that you try to spend a couple of days on site with one or two franchises. A quality franchise company should support these extended interviews because they can be extremely helpful in determining if you and the franchisor are a good match.

Franchise Agreement

In the world of franchising, this is the single most important document you will ever sign. This is why I recommend that you hire an attorney with as much franchise experience as possible. He or she will be able to determine what, if anything, in the agreement can be modified to your advantage. By assessing the franchise agreement, an experienced franchise attorney can also shed some light on the quality of the franchisor—and alert you to any potential risks.

You must also carefully read the agreement, taking note of your obligations, the franchisor's obligations, and remedies to breaches by either party. The agreement term is especially important. A term that is too short (e.g., five years) could give you insufficient time to establish your business. On the other hand, a term that is too long (e.g., 20 years) could subject you to an unfair test of time. Much can change in 20 years, including new ownership of the Franchise Company and adverse industry conditions. Although Medicine Shoppe had a 20-year franchise term, I now believe that a 10-15 year term would have been best.

In addition to the length of the term, it's important to know what happens when the agreement is up. Be sure you thoroughly understand your rights—and the franchisor's rights. Remember, franchisors aren't legally obligated to renew your agreement. And if they do renew, they're not required to provide the same terms and conditions.

It's also essential to know under exactly what conditions you can sell your franchise. Exiting the business can be very restrictive to the franchisee. Generally speaking, most franchisors have a first right of refusal to purchase your franchise when you want to sell. They will also typically retain the right to approve the buyer and require him to attend franchise training, as well as a host of other requirements. Therefore, make sure *you* understand everything contained in the franchise agreement. It's not enough for your attorney to understand these restrictions, since he or she may not be with you ten years from now.

Let's talk a minute about the underlying purpose of a franchise agreement. To ensure uniformity and quality control, franchising imposes a virtually inflexible system for operating the business. These restrictions usually apply to:

- Site approval
- Appearance standards
- Goods and services
- Method of operation
- Sales territory

Many of these requirements may be costly, such as completing periodic renovations or buying only from an approved supplier. They may also restrict your creativity and business judgment. You must be absolutely sure you can live within those limitations before committing to the franchise agreement.

We have not yet discussed franchise fees. Franchisors have two sets of fees: the initial up-front franchise fee and the recurring fee (usually a percentage of gross revenue). The recurring fee (sometimes referred to as a royalty) can be weekly, monthly or quarterly, depending upon the franchisor and the nature of the business. One of the things to put on your due diligence list is to determine how the royalty percentage relates to gross margin and net profit. Here's an example:

1. Product sells for $100.00.

2. Gross Margin is 40% or $40.00.

3. Royalty is 5% of gross sales or $5.00.

4. $5.00 divided by $40.00 equals 13%.

5. 13% of your gross margin is royalty.

6. Let's assume your total cost of completing that sale (overhead, personnel, etc., but not including royalty) is $25.00, leaving a net profit of $15.00 or 15% of the sale.

7. Royalty represents 33.3% of your profit.

Is this royalty too high? It really depends on the franchisor's value proposition. As your partner, the franchisor must contribute enough value to justify receiving 13% of your gross margin and 33.3% of your net profit. Do you see the benefit of doing this calculation? It may by itself govern your decision.

You should also know that you may have to pay recurring royalties even if your franchise hasn't generated proportional income. Additional or miscellaneous royalties (such as those for using the franchise name) may also be required. And all of these fees will be due for the duration of your agreement, even if the franchisor fails to provide promised support services.

As you can see, the franchise agreement's restrictive nature can be both a benefit and a liability. Can you live with the obligations? Can you live with the fees? Are you willing to operate within a defined system of doing business? Are you willing to give up creative license? Only you can determine if the end justifies the means.

I'm not sure that franchisors seek out true entrepreneurs. By definition, entrepreneurs are individualists who like to run their own show. They are usually creative, enjoy making decisions, and are willing to take risks. Before making a decision to buy a franchise—any franchise—re-read "Introduction & Introspection." It will help you determine if you have the unique qualities to become a successful franchisee.

Available Training

As part of the due diligence process, you'll need to carefully evaluate the training program, including ongoing training and additional costs. Typically, franchisee training is conducted at franchise headquarters. The length of the training program depends upon the complexity of the business and specialized knowledge required. For example, restaurant franchise training covers this industry's unique operating systems, food preparation techniques, staffing procedures, etc.

Most franchisors provide additional on-site training before the franchisee's opening. There are no hard and fast rules for assessing a training program and rating its quality. You just need to be sure that it has adequately prepared you for running the business. If you don't have absolute confidence in the training program, you may need to consider another franchise that is better suited to your skills and experience.

One final comment about the due diligence process: Please don't shortchange it. The time and money you spend on the evaluation process will pale in comparison to the hit you could take by choosing the wrong franchise program. By the same token, it can yield great dividends by leading you to the one that's a perfect fit for you!

The Business Plan

By now I'm sure you must be tired of my talking about writing a business plan. However, as discussed previously, having a business plan is absolutely essential before starting a franchise business. A franchise business plan is very similar to one for a new business. The primary difference is the addition of existing data as a basis for your projections. This data can be obtained from the UFOC and your franchisee interviews. The UFOC is also an excellent resource for other elements of your business plan, including corporate history, startup/operating costs, method of operation, marketing plan, etc.

A typical franchise business plan should contain the following informational sections:

- *Introduction* – A comprehensive description of the franchisor and the franchise business.

- *Value Proposition* – Describe the benefits associated with the franchise business and why you believe buying this franchise is the right way to go. In other words, emphasize the franchisor's strengths.*Capital Requirements* – How much are you seeking? Include the structure, depending upon the source of funds.

- *Use of Proceeds* – How you are going to use the money. Remember to include working capital needed to cover early losses.

- *Sources of Revenue* – Identify all revenue sources. *Competition* – This is a question for the franchisor, who knows its competition better than anyone else.

- *Initial startup costs* – This includes the initial franchise fee, cost of training, and opening costs (e.g., leasehold improvements, furniture and fixtures, inventory, operating licenses, insurance, etc.).

- *Financial Plan* – Here again, I believe you should provide three years of projections. Information obtained from existing franchisees can greatly facilitate this process.

- *Operating Plan* – This supports the financial plan. Explain what you expect to do and how that impacts the growth model shown above.

- *Risk Analysis* – Identify the risks, then show how franchisor assistance can mitigate them.

Financing

Most of the sources described in the first section, **"Starting a New Business,"** also apply to buying a franchise. The only exception would be equity financing, unless you can obtain it from family and friends. And this option is recommended only if the business can't support bank debt financing.

The SBA guaranty program is an excellent candidate. Traditional lenders and the SBA like financing franchises due to their built-in management support and industry knowledge. You may also find that the franchisor provides financing. This usually takes the form of equipment leasing, but not always. In any event, you already have enough information on financing strategies from the previous sections, so I won't belabor the point.

Regulations & Requirements

Because franchising is state–regulated, each state may define what constitutes a franchise. For example, some states exclude a business from franchising regulations if there is no up-front fee. Other states have a trademark requirement. However, it's almost universally accepted that if a business exercises significant influence in how the party that is granted distribution rights conducts its affairs, then that business is deemed a franchisor and is subject to regulation. Businesses that escape the franchise designation are known as distributorships and dealerships. These are not regulated under the franchise laws. Typically the franchise agreement is a license agreement and is rather restrictive.

A franchisor must register to do business in each state where it chooses to operate by submitting a Uniform Franchise Offering Circular (UFOC). The UFOC is required of all franchisors by the Federal Trade Commission (FTC). This document is similar to a securities offering, in that it makes various representations and warranties. The UFOC is generally accepted in every state, but there may be some state-specific requirements.

In addition, each time a franchisor wants to make material changes to its operating system or fees, it must submit a new UFOC in the states in which it operates. Gaining state approval can take as long as a year, with the minimum at four to six months.

The UFOC is required to protect the prospective franchisee and is a valuable tool for you to evaluate the business opportunity. It contains detailed information about:

- The Franchisor, its Predecessors and Affiliates
- Business Experience
- Litigation
- Bankruptcy
- Initial Franchise Fee
- Other Fees
- Initial Investment
- Restrictions on Purchase Sources of Products and Services
- Franchisee Obligations
- Franchisor Obligations
- Territory
- Trademarks
- Patents, Copyrights and Proprietary Information
- Financing
- Obligation to Participate in the Operation of the Franchise Business
- Restrictions on What the Franchisee Can Sell
- Renewal, Termination, Transfer and Dispute Resolution

- Public Figures
- Earnings Claims
- List of Franchised Outlets
- Financial statements
- Contracts
- Receipts

Although most of these categories are self-explanatory, there are a few that merit special attention:

Franchise/Other Fees – This includes your initial deposit or franchise fee (which may be non-refundable) and other startup costs (e.g., equipment, signs, initial inventory, etc.). There may also be several undisclosed costs, such as those for business licenses, advertising, insurance, employee salaries/benefits, and legal/accounting fees. Your total estimated costs should include operating expenses for the first year—and living expenses for up to two years.

Earnings Claims – Because franchisors aren't required to make earnings claims, they are rarely included in the UFOC. If a franchisor does make these claims, the FTC requires it to provide written substantiation. In this case, make sure you request the earnings claims document and review it carefully. You should also obtain written materials to support any earnings projections. Be aware that "average incomes," sample earnings, and gross sales (vs. actual profits) can be very misleading.

Territory – Many franchisors offer a protected territory, which can be both an asset and a liability. Although this may restrict competing franchisees, it may also prevent you from opening additional stores or moving to a better location. Make sure you can live within the franchisor's location limits.

Financial Statements – It's essential to have an accountant review the franchisor's financial statements to determine the company's financial strength. You must be absolutely certain your investment will not be at risk due to corporate closing or bankruptcy!

Franchisee/Franchisor Obligations – Make sure you fully understand your legal obligations to the franchisor, as well as theirs to you. Remember, these restrictions are legally binding and carry serious consequences if broken. You should also confirm that the franchise agreement accurately reflects these terms and conditions.

Net Worth

Many franchise companies require their franchisees to have a minimum net worth. This is in direct correlation to the size of investment. Here are some examples:

- A fast-food restaurant franchisor requires a minimum net worth of $2,000,000 with liquid assets of at least $250,000.

- An auto aftermarket franchisor requires a minimum net worth of $200,000, not including equity in the primary residence. Of this amount, $100,000 must be in cash or liquid securities.
- A drive-in restaurant franchisor requires a minimum net worth of $500,000 and liquid assets of $200,000.

Master Franchise License

Some franchisors offer a "Master Franchise License." This gives a franchisee the right to open several franchises within a geographic area, according to a specified schedule. In this case, the master franchisee may or may not be allowed to sub-franchise. If the master license allows for sub-franchising, then the master franchisee becomes a re-seller of the franchise under the same terms and conditions as the original franchise agreement. If sub-franchising is not allowed, then the master franchisee is required to develop his/her own chain of franchises. In both cases, the master franchisee must meet a predetermined development schedule or risk forfeiting the territory and losing whatever monies paid for the Master License.

It should be understood that a Master Franchise License Agreement that provides the right to sub-franchise is essentially a sales tool for the franchisor. It can also be used to insulate the franchisor from direct franchisee liabilities. Although territorial development agreements can occasionally be mutually beneficial, I recommend thorough analysis and evaluation before pursuing this route.

"Simple But Not Stupid" (A few tips on closing sales)

I would like a dollar for all the times people have told me that they hate selling ... or that they can't sell ... or that they're uncomfortable selling.

In every case—and I mean every case—what these individuals are really saying is that they fear rejection. They fear hearing a "no." The fact is that everyone sells something, every single day.

We begin to fear rejection at a very early age. This happened to me in fourth grade, during after-school baseball. The two captains (arguably the best players, or the biggest) would choose their teams. One would say, "I take Billy." The other, "I take Sammy." And on and on it went, until they got to the last boy. "You take Mikey," one captain would shout. "No, you take him; put him in right field," said the other. And off I would trot to right field, feeling very rejected.

For others, perhaps it was the first time you were rejected by a member of the opposite sex. No matter when it happened, the fear of rejection was, to some degree, implanted into our brains.

The most successful salespersons are those who overcome the fear of rejection the most. I say "the most" because I don't believe it's possible to completely overcome our fears. We simply learn to live with them—and turn them to our advantage when necessary.

Every one of us sells something every day. We sell our spouses on doing certain things. We sell our children on how to behave. We sell teachers, employers, and superiors on ourselves. In light of this, I ask you to remove the phrases listed in paragraph one from your vocabulary and emotionally understand that you *can* sell. It's true that some are more articulate and outgoing than others. But the important thing is to learn to play to your strengths. Some of us are what I like to call visual, while others are auditory or tactile. Visual people are more influenced by what they see. Selling to a visual person involves painting a picture. If you're selling to an auditory person, then it's important that he or she hears what you want them to hear. The tactile person is more likely to buy on the strength of touch. While the sales presentation may impact in all three areas, it's important to determine where the emphasis should be placed. Watch for clues about a person's sales type. An individual that comments on a painting in the room is likely to be a visual person. Someone that pays more attention to background music is generally more auditory.

It's important to understand that the easiest decision to make is the decision *not* to buy. This is because that decision doesn't change anything. The status quo remains. Most of us don't like change, and that's why it's easier to say "no." A buying decision requires change, change in the amount of money you have and hopefully, in your quality of life after spending it!

Now let's discuss some of the techniques that can make you a more successful salesperson. Here are some practical examples:

Example 1:

You and your technocrat are making a technology sales presentation to three executives of ABC Company. Among the three are the VP of the IT Department, the VP of Marketing and the CEO. It's quite likely that the personalities of all three are significantly different. Yet you have to play to your audience as a whole. You also have a judgment call to make: Assuming the decision-maker is the CEO, which of the other two has the greatest influence? By making this call, you quickly carve out the roles that you and your associate will play during the presentation.

Mirroring is a great technique when you are meeting with someone. This is done by simply imitating the physical position of the person to whom you are speaking. If he or she is leaning forward with hands clasped on the table, then you assume the same body position. This technique works in all meetings. When interviewing for a job, mirroring the interviewer can greatly improve one's chances of being hired.

The most frequently asked question in technology presentations is "I like what I see, but can you retrofit it to do this and that?" The most common answer to this question (usually coming from the technocrat) is "No, we can't make those changes." This answer is **wrong, wrong, wrong!** This question has been answered with no thought whatsoever. The correct answer is **"I don't have enough information to say yes."** Given enough money, anything is possible. The only question which can't be answered until later is whether the changes will be cost effective.

I've spent a lot of time trying to teach associates that the answer to a question is rarely "no"! A "no" answer can cost you a sale. The correct answer given above can buy you valuable time—and may ultimately win the sale!

Example 2:

You are a sales clerk in a furniture store, and a customer enters. It's always important to appear busy, even if there's no other customer in the store. You should always acknowledge the customer by saying hello and telling her that you'll be right with her. In furniture stores, most everyone wants to look around before zeroing in on what they might purchase. This gives you time to observe and determine where your focus should be. Notice that I designated the customer as a woman. This is because most furniture store customers are female. A male customer is almost always accompanied by his wife.

Sell benefits, not features. All features have corresponding benefits; people buy based on benefits, not features. For example, my wife and I have a "Sleep Number" bed. It *features* a remote control that allows us to choose different degrees of firmness for each side. The *benefit* is that we each have a unique setting that gives us the best possible sleep.

Recognize buying signals. One classic selling mistake is not recognizing buying signals. Some examples of buying signals are: "Do you take credit cards?" "Do you deliver?" "Will I be able to order additional chairs for this table?" When a buying signal is given, stop selling! Move to closing the sale as soon as practical. "Yes, we take MasterCard and Visa; which one will you be using?" Don't oversell! Once a customer has decided to buy, the less said, the better.

Handling objections. The key to successful selling is to focus on one objection at a time. After you've overcome the last objection, you can usually close the sale. Never pass over an objection, because it will inevitably crop up at the end of the selling process and keep you from closing the sale. And don't forget that it's always easier to say "no" than "yes." If you systematically handle every objection, it becomes virtually impossible to say "no."

How to close the sale. There are various ways to close the sale, and many books have been written on the subject. However, every expert will agree that **you must ask for the order.** Many years ago, the CEO of what was then an early-stage company approached a venture capital firm about raising funds. The CEO did a superb job of selling his company. But when the venture capitalist agreed to go forward, the CEO didn't know how to ask for the order! Because he had no idea how much money he needed, he couldn't close the sale.

There are many effective ways to ask for an order. These include:

- Asking the customer how she wants to pay for the merchandise.
- Asking when is the best time to deliver the product.
- Summarizing benefits versus cost.
- Asking the customer if there's any reason why she shouldn't purchase the item.

If the customer says she needs more time to think about it, ask if you can call her at a specific time. If she wants to bring her husband back to the store, try to set a date for that meeting during your work hours.

I consider myself to be a very good salesman. But in all honesty, I can only sell something that I believe in—and can become passionate about. This makes me feel like I'm not really selling, but giving someone a great opportunity.

Some years ago, while I was still with Medicine Shoppe, I lectured at several pharmacy schools on the benefits of owning your own business. When I was at the University of Iowa, a student raised his hand and said, "Mr. Busch, it seems like you're only interested in making money. When I open my drugstore, it's going to be such and such."

My response was, "Young man, I can appreciate what you're saying, but let me ask you a question. Do you believe that you have a service to provide?" He nodded yes. "Well, do you believe that you can provide that service better than others?" Again, he nodded yes. "Then your first obligation to your community is to make a profit, because if you don't make a profit, you won't be around to serve that community. You'll be out of business! Also, when you talk about what your drugstore will look like, I submit that my pharmacies are what my customer wants. I wouldn't locate a Medicine Shoppe in a highly affluent neighborhood, where the community demands charge accounts and delivery. Medicine Shoppes are open from 10 AM to 6 PM, do not deliver, and are 'cash and carry' operations."

Once again, we sell ourselves all of the time. If you're successful selling yourself, then you can be successful selling anything. The key is to be prepared. Know your product and your market "inside out." If someone doesn't realize you're giving them a great opportunity, move on to the next group. Each time you don't close, you still win. The education you gain from your last presentation is invaluable for the next one!

It has been my pleasure and privilege to share my entrepreneurial experiences—both good and bad—with you.

No matter what path you choose, I wish you great success—and sincerely hope this book has been helpful. Be sure to study the Exhibits in the following pages. These "real life" examples will give you a head start on your business venture.

Welcome to the world of business ownership!

Exhibits

Business Plan – prepared March 2000

Small Business Administration Forms (SBA)

Sample Asset Purchase Agreement

CHSI
COMMUNITY HEALTH SERVICES

CHSI CORPORATION BUSINESS PLAN

BUSINESS-TO-BUSINESS (B2B)
AN ASP | PORTAL PHARMACY SOLUTION

INTRODUCTION

CHSI serves as an aggregator of product and service suppliers, a facilitator of a lower cost distribution system, and a direct provider of value-added initiatives to the retail pharmacy marketplace. The CHSI strategy builds upon one fundamental element: connectivity through an application service provider (ASP). By networking pharmacies in a VPN extranet, CHSI adds value, enabling each pharmacy to expand its product and service offerings in a cost efficient manner, resulting in added profitability.

The Company targets an audience of the more than 35,000[1] independently owned and regional chain retail pharmacies. Today, independents serve approximately 27 percent of the market, and regional chains have an estimated 8 percent market share. Collectively, they maintain a detailed patient database of more than 135 million lives. 1999 total industry Rx revenues of $120 billion are predicted to double, generating $240 billion by 2005.

To view this splash page, visit www.goodspider.com/sysgen/chsiasp.

Simply stated, an ASP is a series of computer servers providing unique applications or solutions. The software applications hosted on the ASP servers enable the pharmacy clients to operate more efficiently under a lower cost model. Coupled with value-added programming, CHSI offers pharmacies a winning strategy to enter the digital age.

---

[1] National Community Pharmacists Association (NCPA), June 22, 1999

ASPs, commonly referred to as "connectivity initiatives," are in great demand throughout the healthcare industry, placing CHSI in a unique position. CHSI is the only company that offers such a powerful suite of applications through the Internet, supporting and providing connectivity throughout the entire "value chain": the consumer, prescriber, pharmacy, and insurer. CHSI will design and build its ASP to scale-up, customize rapidly, and deliver the performance, reliability, and availability required in today's pharmacy and healthcare industries.

The Company intends to enter into agreements with each of the major retail pharmacy operating system providers, e.g., ComcoTech, Health Business Systems, McKesson Pharmacy Systems (MPS), National Data Corporation (NDC), and QS1. Such agreements are possible in that CHSI will provide a value added proposition to the software companies whereby they will increase current reoccurring revenues. Under the agreements, CHSI's B2B ASP solution will allow for each participating store's workstations to simultaneously offload a digital image in real-time of each transaction to the ASP host computers while recording the actual transaction to the in-house server. This simple process will allow CHSI to aggregate and data mine all information to and from the switching companies, PBMs, providers and payors.

CHSI combines its e-business ASP and an outside pharmacy fulfillment program with the member store. The ASP will offer a complete web solution, process and adjudicate prescription claims, as well as all other transactions moving through the system. CHSI anticipates the ASP to be developed within 90 days following funding and beta tested for 60 days. Once tested, CHSI will market the fully operational ASP.

CHSI expects its alternative outside prescription fulfillment center to become a significant revenue generator, providing retail mail order, centralized institutional pharmacy, prescription compounding, homeopathic medicines, and additional health and wellness products. Industry demographics dictate the need for a more cost efficient drug dispensing and delivery system; the CHSI model substantially increases each participating pharmacy's market share without increased investment or operating costs.

CHSI brings its business audience into the digital age, changing the future landscape of community pharmacy. Its low cost e-business model presents pharmacies with increased purchasing power, access to institutional customers, an Internet presence, alternative fulfillment programs, professional information management, and a seamless real-time technology interface platform. These offerings directly result in growth at the local pharmacy level and increased revenue and profit for CHSI.

The CHSI link to pharmacies lowers operating costs, increases productivity and strengthens the personal assets of local pharmacists. It not only frees up financial resources, it frees up the storeowners' and pharmacists' time. No longer processors, community pharmacists can concentrate on what they do best – serve their customers.

CHSI's ability to become the premier community pharmacy solutions provider resides in its management and the assimilation of pharmacy information through a secure, reliable and efficient ASP.

VALUE ADDED PROPOSITION

CHSI believes it will achieve a market share of eight percent or 3,000 ASP users by the end of year two and a 15 percent market share representing 5,400 users by the end of year three. CHSI outlines the value-added propositions supporting this projection below:

- Electronic linkage in the pharmacy value chain is a foregone conclusion. Pharmaceutical manufacturers, patients, physicians, pharmacies, PBMs and managed care organizations (MCOs) will all be part of the link. Independent retail pharmacies and smaller chains' must opt to participate in CHSI or a similar model less they risk exclusion from participation.

- CHSI enables the pharmacies to keep pace with burgeoning prescription growth by providing the stores with its three-part outside pharmacy fulfillment program, mitigating the stores' need for additional capital requirement while increasing store profits.

- While all B2B solutions can add value, B2B companies incur high marketing costs to attract "eyeballs". CHSI provides connectivity to its target audience, the pharmacy community. Its ASP applications "zero" in on tools to enable its participating pharmacies to grow market share without a corresponding proportionate investment.

- CHSI anticipates little if any price resistance from pharmacists connecting to the ASP.

REVENUE SOURCES

CHSI will derive its primary revenue from the following sources:

- ASP Transaction Fees: Each transaction over the ASP, whether CHSI acts as a facilitator or as a provider, will result in a transaction fee. While fees may vary according to the transaction, CHSI estimates the average at $0.24. Transaction fees levied for prescriptions will replace maintenance fees, price updates, post adjudication and switch fees currently paid to software providers. In as much as pharmacies will average over 46,000 prescription transactions annually (including modest growth), total transactions should easily exceed 50,000 per store within the first twelve months on the CHSI system. In addition, outside prescription fulfillment (see below) also will generate transaction fees.

- Outside Prescription Fulfillment: Each automatic Rx refill, institutional Rx and compounded Rx filled at the CHSI central fulfillment center will result in a transaction fee charged to the pharmacy as well as direct revenues to CHSI. (See "Outside Prescription Fulfillment," pages 7-12.)

- ASP License Fee: CHSI requires each participating pharmacy to pay a one-time fee of $500. CHSI will install the gateway to its ASP on participating stores' existing technology or will provide pre-programmed network appliances, whichever is appropriate.

- <u>Monthly Service Charge:</u> CHSI charges stores a monthly fee of $195 or $2,340 per year.

- <u>Other:</u> CHSI intends to market accessibility to pharmaceutical manufacturers and other product and service providers.

BUSINESS-TO-BUSINESS INITIATIVE

Once fully developed, CHSI's private and secure ASP will give pharmacies the most cost-efficient link to their industry, directly networking retailers, manufacturers, and vendors, and providing CHSI participating pharmacies with the best prices for a variety of products and services. The ASP system takes costs out of the traditional distribution channel, giving pharmacies more advantageous pricing.

Pharmacists can sell and purchase excess inventory via an online auction, "attend" virtual certified education classes, and take advantage of supplier and service offerings. CHSI will provide online special incentives, training, promotions and forums. Through ASP connectivity, the more than 600,000 physicians nationwide can access supplies at the lowest possible cost through CHSI local participating pharmacies. CHSI will facilitate any value-added product or service, and receive transaction fees for its efforts.

Through real-time information, pharmacies will have the tools to more effectively manage their assets [e.g., increase inventory turns, audit third-party reimbursements, cash management, etc.]. The ASP electronically processes prescription claims, Internet transactions, and enables the pharmacy to fill e-scripts.

CHSI and participating pharmacies will share additional revenues generated from the data mining and drilling of patient health-related information. Proof of drug therapy compliance to third parties and proof of moving market share to manufacturers result in economic benefit. Until now, only the large chains, mail order pharmacies, and institutional providers have been able to take advantage of this opportunity. The CHSI ASP levels the playing field.

BUSINESS-TO-CONSUMER INITIATIVE

The business-to-consumer site in every sense becomes the catalyst for the business-to-business initiative. The consumer site will utilize the web to drive traffic to the store and vice-versa, providing a total solution to the patient. CHSI, by capitalizing on an existing extensive patient database of an average 4,000-5,000 lives per store, generates a low cost customer acquisition model.

Benefiting from the sea of changes made by the early online drug stores and other surfacing ventures, CHSI elected to become both a facilitator and a provider to its consumer initiative. Stores will be able to select their own web vendor for distribution of traditional health and beauty aid (HBA) products with the supply chain linked to the ASP.

The Company will facilitate health information content through the aggregation of well-regarded providers with whom it is currently negotiating relationships. CHSI, through its mail order fulfillment center, will be the site's exclusive provider of pharmacy services. This fulfillment center also will provide consumer access to alternative medicine and wellness products.

The CHSI web strategy calls for the creation of each individual pharmacy's URL, keeping the customer closely tied to his/her preferred pharmacist. Business-to-business, supported by business-to-consumer, gives a digital life to community pharmacy.

OUTSIDE PRESCRIPTION FULFILLMENT: INSTITUTIONAL

The first element of outside pharmacy fulfillment encompasses marketing to institutional prospects on behalf of the individual store. Changes in reimbursement rates, inefficiencies in service provision by the large institutional pharmacy corporations and the growth in assisted-living facilities have created opportunities for a new community pharmacy drive to recapture a significant market share of both the long-term care and the assisted-living markets.

The CHSI strategy positions local store personnel to service the immediate needs of up to 500 patients/residents. The CHSI contracted fulfillment center fills 85 percent of the patient medications under one uniform drug delivery system using a cycle fill schedule. Once filled, the CHSI center delivers back to the stores for distribution to the patient facilities. CHSI identified automation that will enable two pharmacists and two-to-three technicians to service 5,000 patients, representing 35,000 Rxs per month.

By limiting the store to no more than 500 institutional patients, CHSI minimizes store investment and provides a better service model to the facility and its patients. The U.S. long-term care market consists of 1.67 million beds; presently, 4.5 million people reside in 60,000 assisted living facilities. The latter, which is expected to grow by 300 percent over the next three to four years, clearly represents the fastest growing segment of institutional business. CHSI projected growth in institutional pharmacy business is directly attributed to projected patient/resident growth. At end of year three the total population will approach 15 million. CHSI's market penetration is estimated to be less than two percent.

As evidenced in the model on page eight, the addition of 300 patients (beds) jointly serviced by the individual store and CHSI via outside fulfillment adds incremental gross revenue of $612,000 to CHSI and $292,120 in gross income to each store. Net income (pre-tax) to CHSI per 300 beds is projected at $81,089 based upon 100 participating stores.

A CHSI outside fulfillment center can be expected to fill approximately 12,000 prescriptions per day based upon its mix of institutional, compounding and retail prescriptions. Therefore, CHSI will need to build three additional centers during its second year and has budgeted accordingly (See page 16 - " Capital Requirements and Use of Proceeds").

OUTSIDE PRESCRIPTION FULFILLMENT PHARMACY: INSTITUTIONAL MODEL

Assumptions:

1. The revenues are based upon a 300 patient load per store. The target audience is long-term care, assisted living and other institutional populations.
2. Rx sales are $200 per patient per month, $720,000 annually
3. 85% of annual sales are booked to CHSI
4. Outside fulfillment: cost of goods plus professional fee
5. Distribution to stores is 10% of CHSI gross revenue
6. Consulting services are estimated at $2.00 for medical records per patient per month and $50.00 per hour for consultant pharmacy time spent per months
7. In-store revenue from new orders, stat & prn prescriptions
8. Medical Service Records Income is $2.00 per patient per month to CHSI
9. Medical Supplies Sales = $90,000 per 300 patients (booked to CHSI)

300 Beds (Patients)

Income/ Revenue	Impact on a SINGLE STORE	100 STORES	300 STORES	500 STORES
Consultant Service	$14,400			
Supplies & House Stock	$86,400			
CHSI Distributions	$62,821			
In-Store Sales (new,prn,stat)	$128,500			
Total Income	$292,120			
Total Rx Sales		$61,201,000	$183,603,000	$306,000,000
Med. Services		$ 720,000	$ 2,160,000	$ 3,600,000
Med. Supplies		$ 900,000	$ 2,700,000	$ 4,500,000
Total Sales		$62,821,000	$188,463,000	$314,100,000
Less Fulfillment		(44,300,000)	(132,900,000)	(221,500,000)
Net Revenue		$18,521,000	$ 55,563,000	$ 92,600,000
Less Store Distributions		(6,282,100)	(18,846,300)	(31,410,000)
Income to CHSI		$12,238,900	$ 36,716,700	$ 61,190,000
CHSI Expenses		(4,130,000)	(11,320,000)	(18,506,000)
CHSI EBITDA		$ 8,108,900	$ 25,396,700	$ 42,684,000
Prescriptions Per Year**	25,200	2,520,000	7,560,000	12,600,000

OUTSIDE PRESCRIPTION FULFILLMENT PHARMACY: COMPOUNDING

This fulfillment program, which creates custom medications for patients, centers on the doctor-patient-pharmacist relationship. In a traditional compounding environment, the patient, who suffers from an ailment, visits the doctor who prescribes the non-commercial solution; the patient then goes to the pharmacy, where the pharmacist creates the prescription according to an often complicated and very exact chemical equation. Sometimes, it is the pharmacist that "invents" the formula and markets it to doctors.

Either way, compounding results in loyal customers and repeat business. They are loyal because, unlike name brand or generic drugs distributed nationally, these medications are unique. By issuing compounded medications in 30-day or fewer supplies, CHSI guarantees built-in customer demand and a steady revenue stream. In the model on page seven, CHSI projects 1440 participating pharmacies in the compounding program by end of year two. This translates into $35.6 million in revenue, with an operating income of $8.6 million to CHSI. By the end of year three, 2,880 pharmacies generate revenues of $126 million and operating income is $45.8 million. Approximately 80 percent of all independent retail pharmacies do some prescription compounding; few chains provide compounding. Approximately 15 percent of the stores purchased a franchise that provides both physician marketing assistance and formulary services. Notwithstanding, compounding requires additional investment in pharmacists and technicians, requires outside marketing and a genuine commitment to successful implementation.

CHSI regional specialists will market "compounding" directly to physicians in the local marketplace and the pharmacy will promote to consumers. The margin in compounding approaches 60 percent, far more lucrative than the 24 percent average margin on commercial prescriptions. CHSI projected revenues identified above is attributable to new business generated from this systematic marketing approach and central mail order fulfillment. Pharmacies can enter the compounding arena without investment or local prescription compounding requirements. They simply serve as the patient conduit.

OUTSIDE PRESCRIPTION FULFILLMENT PHARMACY: COMPOUNDING MODEL

Assumptions:

1. Number of Rx per Pharmacy:
   - First year of operation: 20 in Quarter 1; 180 in Quarter 2; 240 in Quarter 3; and 360 in Quarter 4 totaling 900 per year.
   - Second year of operation: 30 per week totaling 1,440 per year
   - Third year of operation: 40 per week totaling 1,920 per year

2. Average Rx Price: $50.00 (all cash)

3. Average Gross Profit: $28.00, a 56% margin (Profit determined as selling price minus costs of goods, labor and delivery.)

4. Distribution to Pharmacy: Approx. 14% of Gross Revenue, equaling $7.00 per average Rx

5. CHSI Marketing Costs: $5,000 per store first full year of participation

	End of Year 2	End of Year 3
Participating Stores	1440	2880
Rx Total Revenues	$35,640,000	$126,360,000
Cost of Sales	(15,681,600	(55,598,400
Gross Profit	$19,958,400	$70,761,600
Distribution to Store	$4,989,600	$17,690,400
Sales & Marketing Costs	$6,300,000	$7,200,000
Net Operating Income	$8,668,800	$45,871,200

OUTSIDE PRESCRIPTION FULFILLMENT PHARMACY: RETAIL

CHSI considers outside fulfillment services an essential element to its internal growth plan for several reasons. First, approximately 20 percent of all consumer prescriptions currently are filled by mail. This trend predominantly is driven by the advent of managed care, but also includes an abundance of prescriptions from Medicare patients.

While managed care organizations negotiate mail order contracts separately, patients under the various plans either can choose a mail order option or go to a listed retail pharmacy provider. Medicare recipients without prescription coverage enjoy total freedom of choice.

CHSI's retail fulfillment, commonly referred to as an automatic refill prescription program, fills the need generated by the rising prescription rates resulting from aging baby boomers. In order to keep pace with growth forecasts, independent community pharmacies require a more efficient and cost effective dispensing method. Outside fulfillment eliminates the costly investment that stores must make to keep pace, producing greater store profits.

CHSI developed a comprehensive program to provide its stores with an alternative retail pharmacy fulfillment option. This is a designated customer 30-day authorized supply automatic refill program on maintenance medications to be sent directly to the customer by mail. CHSI retains the right to agree to provide fulfillment services depending upon the reimbursement conditions of any third party contract.

Approximately 60 percent of all prescriptions filled are classified as maintenance medications, those drugs generally taken on a regular long-term cycle. CHSI alternative retail fulfillment is projected to capture less than 15 percent first year market share (maintenance Rxs only) from each of its participating pharmacies, under 20 percent after two years and less than 30 percent in year three.

OUTSIDE PRESCRIPTION FULFILLMENT PHARMACY: RETAIL MODEL

Assumptions:

1. CHSI fulfillment center receives authorization from pharmacy to refill a patient prescription and the center fills the prescription in accordance with state laws and mails to the patient following notification that the adjudication has taken place.

2. Average store fills 38,000 Rxs per year.

3. CHSI estimates 9% mail order rate first full year, 14% rate year two & 20% rate year three without consideration of pharmacy growth.

4. Gross margin to CHSI after fulfillment is 9%.

5. Average Rx is $38.00, 4% of revenue to stores.

6. EBITDA to CHSI is 5% of gross revenue.

	300 stores	1500 stores	2700 stores
	Year 1	Year 2	Year 3
Total Rx Sales	$9,849,600	$14,774,400	$147,744,000
Single Store Revenue	$1,641	$8,208	$11,491
Net Revenue EBITDA CHSI	$492,480	$738,720	$7,387,200

POTENTIAL COMPETITION

In as much as there are no barriers of entry in building an ASP, CHSI recognizes the importance of understanding the industry and predicting from where competition may arise. Currently, CHSI identifies two obvious possibilities: software providers and wholesale drug distributors.

While the pharmacy software system providers can easily build an ASP, by nature they only provide the pharmacy application and lack all of the other value-added elements included in the CHSI model. As a result, there is little reason pharmacies with the software provider's stand-alone operating system will link to the same company's ASP.

Wholesale drug distributors may attempt to develop an ASP-hybrid somewhat similar to CHSI. These companies, however, will face several challenges developing this type of initiative. First of all, all distributors leave a trail of historical proof detailing their inability to successfully implement programs far a field from their core business. Secondly, few independent pharmacies will permit supplier access to such detailed patient data. Third, distributors are not likely to undertake outside fulfillment programs likened to the CHSI model.

CHSI has projected aggressive growth to 5,400 ASP users (approximately 15.5 percent market share) by the end of year three. This targeted growth is supported by capital needs in of $12 million in year one, $31.6 million in year two and $19.6 million in year three. This investment helps to insure CHSI market penetration. Once stores are linked to the CHSI ASP there is no likely reason for a switch to that of a competitor. Unless of course, CHSI does not sustain its value added proposition.

PHARMACY MARKETING

CHSI will first market to the pharmacy software vendors' 10,000 customers. With the second phase, CHSI will expand its focus to the entire universe of 35,000 pharmacies. CHSI will give special emphasis to the myriad of cooperative buying groups that attempt to leverage themselves. Access to real-time data will be especially attractive to such organizations: information equals clout.

CHSI's marketing program will implement the following strategies, either independently or together with another health-related vendor:

- Regional sales presentations, captivating the audience at locations where they cannot be distracted by other events
- Exhibiting and participating in medical and pharmacy association trade shows
- Public and media relations
- Executive visibility and strategic networking – placing key executive spokespersons on select medical, technology, business and financial panels
- Direct mail and e-mail campaigns
- Advertising in trade publications and in tradeshow brochures
- Strategic advertising in trade publications and related Internet sites
- Sponsor industry-related events, or "piggy-back" off existing ones by scheduling a CHSI event the day before
- Personal sales through regional CHSI representatives

TARGETING SUPPLIERS & AFFINITY GROUPS

Physicians: Through its regional representatives in each network market, CHSI will directly market prescription compounding and the sale of physician supplies. CHSI will target prescribers including physicians, podiatrists and veterinarians, via email, personal physician visits, and direct mail.

Institutions: CHSI will pursue institutions, including long-term care facilities and assisted living residences. The Company will secure contracts under CHSI's Institutional Prescription Fulfillment Model outlined on page seven.

Vendors & Suppliers: CHSI will market its business-to-business initiative to suppliers and vendors who may wish to offer special incentives, products, services or content on the web site. In this role, CHSI will act as a facilitator to these companies. As previously stated, CHSI will remain the sole outside prescription service provider.

CORPORATE POSITIONING

Media & Public Relations: CHSI will promote itself, its management team, and member networks to local media, as well as to the national business and trade press. The Company will create case studies highlighting the strengths of the program appeal to the different pharmacy owner profiles. In addition, the company will focus on executive visibility through its presence at business and industry forums, trade shows, and other speaking platforms. CHSI will also research the benefit of sponsorship opportunities, promotions, and special events.

Investor Relations & Market Intelligence: As CHSI explores its future options to become a publicly traded company, it will expand its marketing department to include sophisticated investor relations consulting and diligent market intelligence research. The Company will consider incorporating conference calls and road shows. The CHSI Board of Directors, with direction from the CEO and outside consultants, will determine the timeline and procedure as that time approaches.

CAPITAL REQUIREMENTS AND USE OF PROCEEDS

The company seeks $12 million in equity financing

USE OF PROCEEDS

Design & Build-Out ASP & All Applications (including content)	$4,500,000
Build-out, equip & stock Fulfillment Center	$4,000,000
Program Marketing	$2,000,000
Working Capital	$3,000,000
	$13,500,000
Less lease/financing	(1,500,000)
	$12,000,000

ADDITIONAL CAPITAL REQUIREMENTS

Year two:	ASP upgrade	$ 4,000,000
	Installation & Training	4,800,000
	Technology upgrades	4,800,000
	Build 3 new fulfillment Centers	18,000,000
		$31,600,000
Year three:	ASP upgrade	$ 5,000,000
	Installation & Training	4,800,000
	Technology upgrades	4,800,000
	Fulfillment Centers Upgrade	10,000,000
		$24,600,000

The Company will seek to complete additional financings to convert its debt into equity.

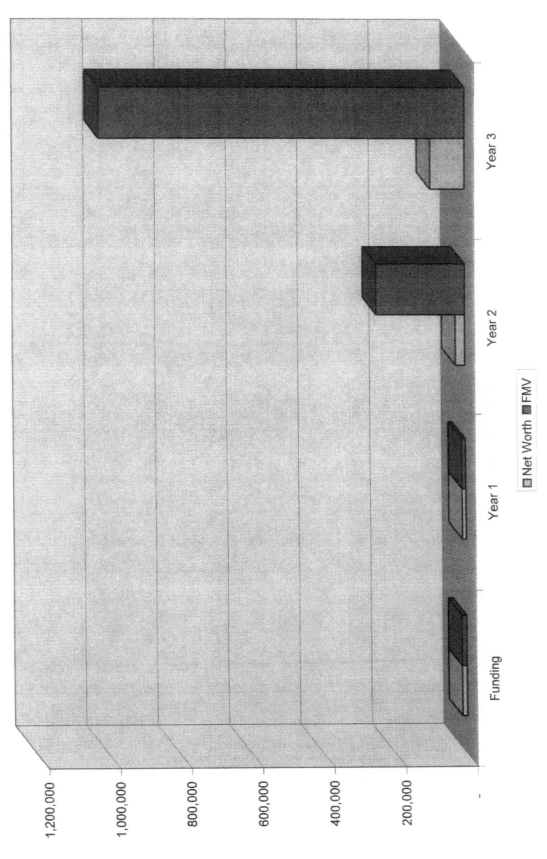

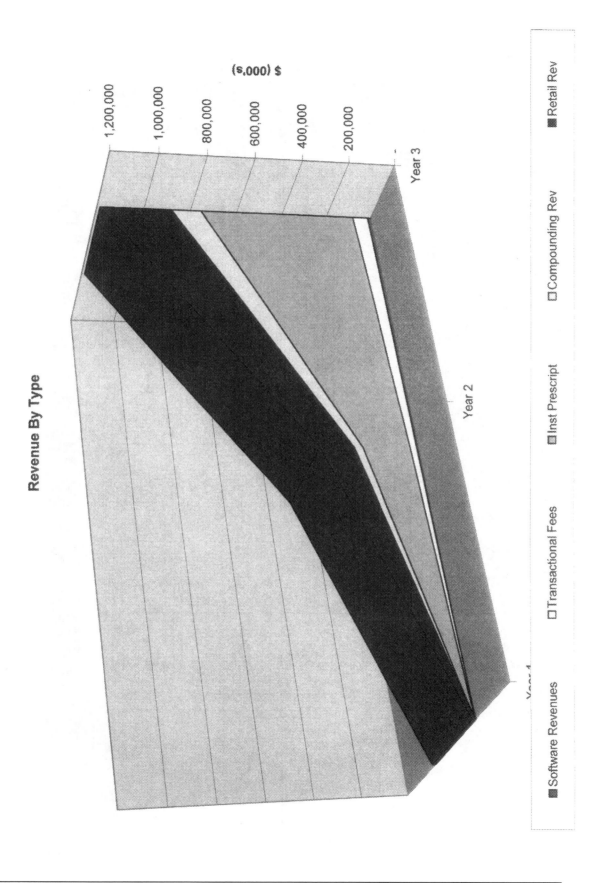

Sales Growth

Revenue By Type

(s,000) $

1,200,000
1,000,000
800,000
600,000
400,000
200,000

Year 3

Year 2

Software Revenues   Transactional Fees   Inst Prescript   Compounding Rev   Retail Rev

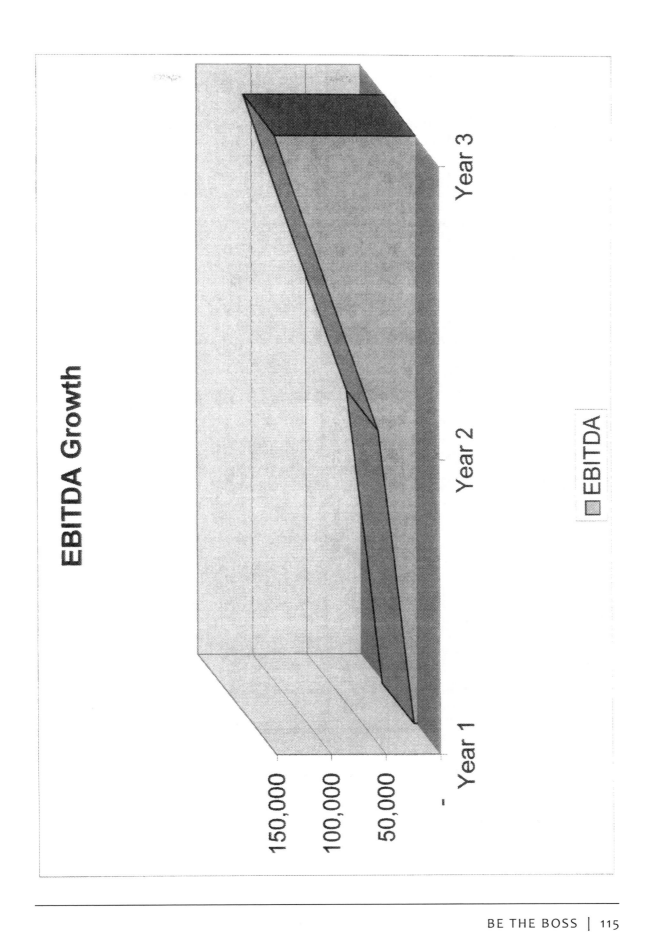

Chairman – James R. Boris: Mr. Boris, former EVEREN Securities chairman and CEO, brings to CHSI more than thirty years of leadership in financial and securities markets. Through a leveraged ESOP in September 1995, Mr. Boris led an employee buyout of Kemper Securities from Kemper Corporation and changed the name to EVEREN. In October 1996, following an IPO, EVEREN Capital Corporation was listed on the New York Stock Exchange. He served as its chairman and CEO until October 1999, when EVEREN was acquired by Charlotte, North Carolina-based First Union Bank Corporation in a transaction valued at $1.2 billion. The newly combined company is the nation's sixth largest securities firm. From 1989 through 1995, he was chairman & CEO of Kemper Securities, Inc. Mr. Boris previously held the positions of executive vice president and director of PaineWebber, Inc. and Shearson Lehman Brothers, Inc

Chief Executive Officer – Michael Busch: Mr. Busch was formerly the CEO of The Wharton Capital Group, a consulting firm engaged in capital access and financial consulting to small- and medium-sized businesses. From 1994 to 1998, Wharton successfully restructured and refinanced $150 million of revenue based retail pharmacies. He is the founder and a former CEO of Medicine Shoppe International, Inc., a company that operates more than twelve hundred franchised pharmacies. Cardinal Health, Inc. (NYSE:CAH) acquired Medicine Shoppe several years ago in a transaction valued at approximately $350 million. Mr. Busch also served as general manager of all non-food divisions for Fox Industries, Inc., a regional wholesale grocery conglomerate with then annual revenues estimated at $400 million.

President & Chief Operating Officer – James C. Greenfield: Mr. Greenfield served as the president & chief operating officer of The Wharton Capital Group since 1991. Mr. Greenfield directed Wharton's pharmacy turnaround activities. Prior to 1991, he held senior level marketing, distribution and managerial positions with Baxter Laboratories and Parke-Davis/Warner Lambert Companies.

Chief Technology Officer (interim) – Raphael Feldman: Currently, Mr. Feldman is the president & CEO of Sysgen Data, Ltd., a web strategy and solutions company. Mr. Feldman possesses substantial expertise in both healthcare and the web. He has advised numerous public and private companies in web strategy and solutions including, more recently, Planet Rx.com and EMD.com (a subsidiary of BioShield).

Executive Vice President, Sales and Marketing – John Kogut: Mr. Kogut most recently served as president of Health Mart, a pharmacy franchise with approximately 850 stores. From 1990 to 1995, he was president & COO of Fay's Drugstore Division, a 277-store chain recently acquired by J.C. Penney and incorporated into its Eckerd drug subsidiary. Net income under his watch grew from $5.9 million on revenues of $500 million in 1990, to $12.6 million on revenues of $921 million in 1995. Mr. Kogut is a pharmacist by profession and a former member of the New York State Board of Pharmacy.

Vice President, Pharmacy Support Services – David Goot: A registered pharmacist, Mr. Goot sold his extensive long-term, compounding and retail pharmacy businesses in 1998 to Pharmerica. He has significant expertise in institutional pharmacy operations and prescription compounding.

Director of Sales, Northwest Region – Gary Damiano: Mr. Damiano, a pharmacist, formerly operated four successful pharmacies. He remains very active in regional pharmacy association activities and is well known in pharmacy circles. He served as past president of United Drug's board of directors.

Director of Sales, Northeast Region – Michael Samale: A registered pharmacist with more than 30 years experience in institutional and retail pharmacy operations, Mr. Samale served in senior management positions with Paid Prescriptions, a subsidiary of Merck-Medco and McKesson Corporation.

ADDITIONAL STAFFING REQUIREMENTS:

CHSI will require a production and design team of approximately six-to-eight people to support its ASP. It also will need to build an e-business development group of two-to-three people to effectuate joint ventures and strategic alliances.

The Company will ramp up to a full compliment of 48 technology installers/trainers by mid-year two.

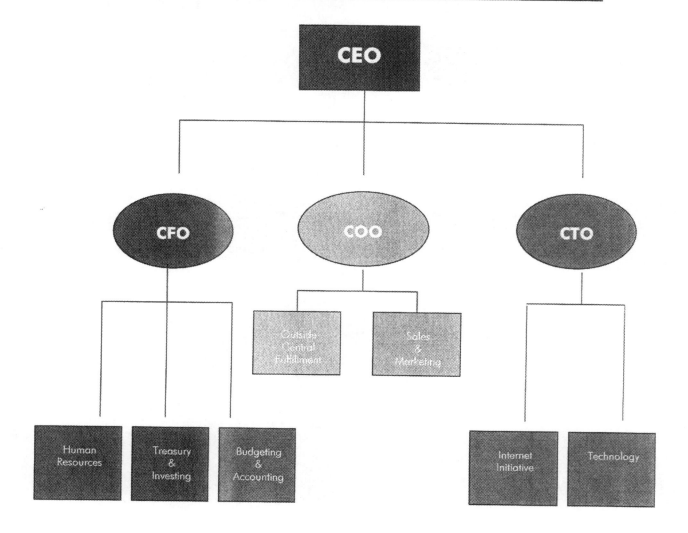

CURRENT CAPITALIZATION (as of 03-03-2000)

[1]Shares Issued and Outstanding

	Shares
James R. Boris	100,000
Michael Busch	1,200,000
James C. Greenfield	1,200,000
John Kogut	1,200,000
Health Business Systems, Inc.	1,000,000
Sysgen Data, Ltd.	300,000
Directors and Beneficial Owners of 5 percent (or more) Issued and Outstanding:	5,000,000
26 Other Shareholders as a Group:	995,000
Total Shares Issued and Outstanding:	5,995,000
Total Options Granted	2,675,000
Total Shares:	**8,670,000**

---

[1] All shareholders holding a beneficial interest of in excess of 5 percent are so noted

CHSI
(000's Omitted)

Proforma Cash Flow Statement

	Year 1	Year 2	Year 3
Cash Flow From Operations:			
Net Income:	(2,844)	15,490	69,306
Depreciation/Amortization	1,895	7,174	11,390
Decreases (Increases) in Accounts Receivable	(1,163)	(30,952)	(60,167)
Decreases (Increases) in Inventory	(603)	(8,842)	(10,721)
Decreases (Increases) in Prepaid Expenses	142	(1,990)	(3,868)
Increases (Decreases) in Accounts Payable	421	11,899	22,549
Increases (Decreases) in Accrued Expenses	616	7,894	14,451
Changes in Other Assets/Liab	-	-	-
Cash Provided By Operations	(1,535)	673	42,940
Investing Activities:			
Capital Expenditures	(9,700)	(29,800)	(23,800)
Financing Activities:			
Dividends Paid	-	-	-
Debt Paydown:			
Senior Debt	-	-	-
Subordinated Debt	-	-	-
Cash Used in Financing Activities	-	-	-
Change in Cash After Debt Reduction	(11,235)	(29,127)	19,140
Revolver Repayment			(11,140)
Revolver Drawdown	23	30,127	
Net Change in Revolver	23	30,127	(11,140)
Net Change in Cash	(11,212)	1,000	8,000

March Financials

4/14/00

CHSI
(000's Omitted)

Proforma Income Statement

	Proforma		
	Year 1	Year 2	Year 3
Revenue	14,948	412,902	1,186,476
Cost of Sales	10,346	295,924	837,105
Gross Profit	4,602	116,978	349,371
Gross Margins	30.8%	28.3%	29.4%
Store Revenue Sharing	545	30,622	97,323
Fufillment Marketing	2,400	13,800	20,700
Sales, General & Administrative Expenses	4,500	38,208	102,235
EBITDA	(2,843)	34,348	129,112
Operating Margins	-19.0%	8.3%	10.9%
Other Income/Expense:			
Other Income	-	-	-
Interest - LOC	1	1,358	2,212
Interest - Note	-	-	-
Interest - Subordinated	-	-	-
Depreciation	1,895	7,174	11,390
Amortization			
Pretax Income	(4,739)	25,816	115,510
Pretax Margins	-31.7%	6.3%	9.7%
Income Tax Expense	(1,896)	10,326	46,204
Net Income	(2,844)	15,490	69,306

4/14/00

The following pages include:

- Proforma Balance Sheet
- Proforma Income Statement
- Proforma Cash Flow Statement
- Detailed Projected Cash Flows
- Proforma Assumptions
- Depreciation Schedule
- Projected Revenues
- Company Valuation
- Appendix – Charts
  Shareholder Value
  Sales Growth
  EBITDA Growth

THIS MATERIAL IS PRESENTED FOR DISCUSSION PURPOSES ONLY AND IS NOT AN OFFERING OF SECURITIES. ANY OFFERING OF SECRUTIES WILL BE MADE ONLY BY A CURRENT CONFIDENTIAL INVESTMENT MEMORANDUM. THE REPRODUCTION AND/OR DISTRIBUTION OF THIS MATERIAL IS STRICTLY FORBIDDEN.

CHSI BALANCE SHEET – (unaudited): December 31, 1999

Assets:

Cash	$190,028
CD on Deposit	22,068
Prepaid Expenses	216,698
Total Current Assets	428,888
Pharmacy Operating Software	<u>1,000,000</u>
Total Assets	1,428,888

Liabilities and Stockholders' Equity:

Accrued Expenses	165,500
Accounts Payable	9,750
Advances from Others	
Total Current Liabilities	175,250
Stockholders' Equity (Deficit):	1,253,638
Common Stock: $.01 par value, 10,000,000 Shares authorized; 4,060,000 and 5,870,000 shares outstanding at 1998 and 1999, respectively	58,700
Additional Paid-In Capital	1,884,385
Accumulated Deficit	(689,447)
Total Stockholders' Equity (Deficit)	1,194,938
Total Liabilities and Stockholders' Equity	$1,428,888

CHSI
(000's Omitted)

Proforma Balance Sheet

	At Funding	Year 1	Year 2	Year 3
Cash	12,212	1,000	2,000	10,000
Accounts Receivable		1,163	32,115	92,281
Inventory		603	9,445	20,166
Prepaids	217	75	2,065	5,932
ST Assets	12,429	2,840	45,624	128,380
Property, Plant & Equipment	1,000	8,805	31,430	43,840
Other Long Term Assets	-	-	-	-
Intangible Assets				
Total Assets	13,429	11,645	77,054	172,220
	0	0	0	0
Accounts Payable	10	431	12,330	34,879
Accrued Liabilities	166	782	8,676	23,127
Senior Debt:				
Line of Credit		23	30,149	19,009
Senior Term Debt		-	-	-
Subordinated Debt		-	-	-
Shareholder Equity:				
Management	1,942	1,942	1,942	1,942
Equity Partner	12,000	12,000	12,000	12,000
Retained Earnings	(689)	(3,533)	11,957	81,263
Total Capital	13,253	10,409	25,899	95,205
Total Liabilities & Owner's Equity	13,429	11,645	77,054	172,220
	0	0	0	0

CHSI
Projected Cash Flows

	Year 1				Total Year 1	Year 2	Year 3
	1st Quarter	2nd Quarter	3rd Quarter	4th Quarter			
Revenues:							
Software Revenues	-	-	475,500	651,000	1,126,500	7,314,000	12,930,000
Transactional Fee Revenue			962,208	1,929,600	2,891,808	27,936,036	67,657,968
Institutional Prescription Revenues						199,192,500	674,190,000
Compounding Revenues				1,080,000	1,080,000	35,640,000	126,360,000
Rx Retail Revenue (Mail order)				9,849,600	9,849,600	142,819,200	305,337,600
Total Revenue	-	-	1,437,708	13,510,200	14,947,908	412,901,736	1,186,475,568
Cost of Sales							
Transactional Software Costs			432,994	868,320	1,301,314	12,571,216	30,446,086
Institutional Prescription Cost of Sales				-	-	143,418,600	485,416,800
Compounding Cost of Sale				475,200	475,200	15,681,600	55,598,400
Rx Retail Cost of Goods				8,569,152	8,569,152	124,252,704	265,643,712
Total Cost of Sales	-	-	432,994	9,912,672	10,345,666	295,924,120	837,104,998
Gross Profit	-	-	1,004,714	3,597,528	4,602,242	116,977,616	349,370,570
			69.9%	26.6%	30.8%	28.3%	29.4%
Store Revenue Sharing							
Institutional (10% of Institutional revenues)	-	-	-	-	-	19,919,250	67,419,000
Compounding (14% of compounding revenues)	-	-	-	151,200	151,200	4,989,600	17,690,400
Retail Mail Order (4% of Retail Revenue)	-	-	-	393,984	393,984	5,712,768	12,213,504
Fulfillment Marketing							
Compounding Sales & Marketing			-	900,000	900,000	6,300,000	7,200,000
Rx Direct Marketing Costs			-	1,500,000	1,500,000	7,500,000	13,500,000
Store Training & IT Installation Expense	-	-	600,000	600,000	1,200,000	4,800,000	4,800,000
Selling, General & Administrative							
Institutional G&A Costs			-	-	-	11,951,550	40,451,400
General & Administrative	625,000	625,000	625,000	625,000	2,500,000	26,256,516	61,783,834
Marketing Expense	500,000	500,000	500,000	500,000	2,000,000		
Total Sales General & Administrative	1,125,000	1,125,000	1,125,000	1,125,000	4,500,000	38,208,066	102,235,234
Earnings Before Interest, Depreciation & Interest	(1,125,000)	(1,125,000)	(720,286)	(1,072,656)	(4,042,942)	29,547,931	124,312,432
EBITDA %			-50.1%	-7.9%	-27.0%	7.2%	10.5%

CHSI
(000's Omitted)

Proforma Operating Assumptions

	Year 1	Year 2	Year 3
Purchase Discounts - (Other Income)	0.0%	0.0%	0.0%
A/R DSO	28.00	28.00	28.00
Prepaid as a % of Sales	0.5%	0.5%	0.5%
Inventory Turns	15.00	30.00	40.00
Long Term Assets (% of Sales)	0.0%	0.0%	0.0%
A/P Days	15.00	15.00	15.00
Accrued Liabilities % of Operating Costs	10.5%	10.5%	10.5%
Minumum Cash Balance	1,000	2,000	10,000
LOC Interest Rate	9.0%	9.0%	9.0%
Senior Term Interest Rate	9.5%	9.5%	9.5%
Subordinated Interest Rate	12.0%	12.0%	12.0%
Fixed/Contingent Management Fee	-	-	-
Total Management Fee	-	-	-
Senior Debt Amortization			
Subordinated Debt Amortization	-	-	-
Equity Distributions (Return of Capital)	-	-	-
Capital Expenditures:			
ASP Development & Upgrades	4,500	4,000	4,000
Fufillment Centers	4,000	18,000	10,000
Store Technology	1,200	4,800	4,800
Other Capital Expenditures		3,000	5,000
Total Capital Expenditures	9,700	29,800	23,800
Income Tax Rate	40.0%	40.0%	40.0%

March Financials

4/14/00

CHSI
(000's Omitted)

Depreciation Schedule

Original PPE	1,000	1,000	1,000	1,000	1,000	1,000	1,000
1st Year Cap Exp	9,700	9,700	9,700	9,700	9,700	9,700	
2nd Year Cap Exp		29,800	29,800	29,800	29,800	29,800	
3rd Year Cap Exp			23,800	23,800	23,800	23,800	
4th Year Cap Exp				-	-		
5th Year Cap Exp							
6th Year Cap Exp							
7th Year Cap Exp							
	10,700	40,500	64,300	64,300	64,300	64,300	64,300
5 year Property 60.0%	1,284	4,860	7,716	7,716	7,716	7,716	7,716
7 year Property 40.0%	611	2,314	3,674	3,674	3,674	3,674	3,674

Software Revenues

	First Quarter	Second Quarter	Third Quarter	Fourth Quarter	Total
Number of Stores	0	0	300	300	600
Year One	$0.00	$0.00	$475,500.00	$651,000.00	$1,126,500.00
Number of Stores	600	600	600	600	3000
Year Two	$1,302,000.00	$1,653,000.00	$2,004,000.00	$2,355,000.00	$7,314,000.00
Number of Stores	600	600	600	600	5400
Year Three	$2,706,000.00	$3,057,000.00	$3,408,000.00	$3,759,000.00	$12,930,000.00

Transaction Fee Revenue

Year One

	First Quarter	Second Quarter	Third Quarter	Fourth Quarter	Total
New Stores Added	0	0	300	300	600
Store Level	0	0	3,750,000	7,500,000	11,250,000
	$0.00	$0.00	$900,000.00	$1,800,000.00	$2,700,000.00
Institutional	0	0	0	0	0
	$0.00	$0.00	$0.00	$0.00	$0.00
Compounding	0	0	0	21,600	21,600
	$0.00	$0.00	$0.00	$5,184.00	$5,184.00
Retail	0	0	259,200	518,400	777,600
	$0.00	$0.00	$62,208.00	$124,416.00	$186,624.00
Total Transactions	0	0	4,009,200	8,040,000	12,049,200
Total Revenue	$0.00	$0.00	$962,208.00	$1,929,600.00	$2,891,808.00
Software Fees	$0.00	$0.00	($432,993.60)	($868,320.00)	($1,301,313.60)
CHSI Revenue	$0.00	$0.00	$529,214.40	$1,061,280.00	$1,590,494.40

Year Two

	First Quarter	Second Quarter	Third Quarter	Fourth Quarter	Total
New Stores Added	600	600	600	600	3000
Store Level	15,000,000	22,500,000	31,500,000	39,000,000	108,000,000
	$3,600,000.00	$5,400,000.00	$7,560,000.00	$9,360,000.00	$25,920,000.00
Institutional	3,150	6,300	12,600	18,900	40,950
	$756.00	$1,512.00	$3,024.00	$4,536.00	$9,828.00
Compounding	54,000	118,800	216,000	324,000	712,800
	$12,960.00	$28,512.00	$51,840.00	$77,760.00	$171,072.00
Retail	1,036,800	1,555,200	2,203,200	2,851,200	7,646,400
	$248,832.00	$373,248.00	$528,768.00	$684,288.00	$1,835,136.00
Total Transactions	16,093,950	24,180,300	33,931,800	42,194,100	116,400,150
Total Revenue	$3,862,548.00	$5,803,272.00	$8,143,632.00	$10,126,584.00	$27,936,036.00
Software Fees	($1,738,146.60)	($2,611,472.40)	($3,664,634.40)	($4,556,962.80)	($12,571,216.20)
CHSI Revenue	$2,124,401.40	$3,191,799.60	$4,478,997.60	$5,569,621.20	$15,364,819.80

Year Three

	First Quarter	Second Quarter	Third Quarter	Fourth Quarter	Total
New Stores Added	600	600	600	600	5400
Store Level	52,500,000	60,000,000	69,750,000	77,250,000	259,500,000
	$12,600,000.00	$14,400,000.00	$16,740,000.00	$18,540,000.00	$62,280,000.00
Institutional	25,200	31,500	37,800	44,100	138,600
	$6,048.00	$7,560.00	$9,072.00	$10,584.00	$33,264.00
Compounding	453,600	583,200	712,800	950,400	2,700,000
	$108,864.00	$139,968.00	$171,072.00	$228,096.00	$648,000.00
Retail	3,628,800	4,406,400	5,313,600	6,220,800	19,569,600
	$870,912.00	$1,057,536.00	$1,275,264.00	$1,492,992.00	$4,696,704.00
Total Transactions	56,607,600	65,021,100	75,814,200	84,465,300	281,908,200
Total Revenue	$13,585,824.00	$15,605,064.00	$18,195,408.00	$20,271,672.00	$67,657,968.00
Software Fees	($6,113,620.80)	($7,022,278.80)	($8,187,933.60)	($9,122,252.40)	($30,446,085.60)
CHSI Revenue	$7,472,203.20	$8,582,785.20	$10,007,474.40	$11,149,419.60	$37,211,882.40

Institutional Revenues

Year One

	First Quarter	Second Quarter	Third Quarter	Fourth Quarter	Totals
New Stores Added	0	0	0	0	0
Total Sales	$0.00	$0.00	$0.00	$0.00	$0.00
Less Fulfillment	$0.00	$0.00	$0.00	$0.00	$0.00
Operating Revenue	$0.00	$0.00	$0.00	$0.00	$0.00
Store Distributions	$0.00	$0.00	$0.00	$0.00	$0.00
Income	$0.00	$0.00	$0.00	$0.00	$0.00
Fulfillment G & A	$0.00	$0.00	$0.00	$0.00	$0.00
EBITDA Net Income	$0.00	$0.00	$0.00	$0.00	$0.00

Year Two

	First Quarter	Second Quarter	Third Quarter	Fourth Quarter	Totals
New Stores Added	150	150	300	300	900
Total Sales	$15,322,500.00	$30,645,000.00	$61,290,000.00	$91,935,000.00	$199,192,500.00
Less Fulfillment	($11,032,200.00)	($22,064,400.00)	($44,128,800.00)	($66,193,200.00)	($143,418,600.00)
Operating Revenue	$4,290,300.00	$8,580,600.00	$17,161,200.00	$25,741,800.00	$55,773,900.00
Store Distributions	($1,532,250.00)	($3,064,500.00)	($6,129,000.00)	($9,193,500.00)	($19,919,250.00)
Income	$2,758,050.00	$5,516,100.00	$11,032,200.00	$16,548,300.00	$35,854,650.00
Fulfillment G & A	($919,350.00)	($1,838,700.00)	($3,677,400.00)	($5,516,100.00)	($11,951,550.00)
EBITDA Net Income	$1,838,700.00	$3,677,400.00	$7,354,800.00	$11,032,200.00	$23,903,100.00

Year Three

	First Quarter	Second Quarter	Third Quarter	Fourth Quarter	Totals
New Stores Added	300	300	300	300	2100
Total Sales	$122,580,000.00	$153,225,000.00	$183,870,000.00	$214,515,000.00	$674,190,000.00
Less Fulfillment	($88,257,600.00)	($110,322,000.00)	($132,386,400.00)	($154,450,800.00)	($485,416,800.00)
Operating Revenue	$34,322,400.00	$42,903,000.00	$51,483,600.00	$60,064,200.00	$188,773,200.00
Store Distributions	($12,258,000.00)	($15,322,500.00)	($18,387,000.00)	($21,451,500.00)	($67,419,000.00)
Income	$22,064,400.00	$27,580,500.00	$33,096,600.00	$38,612,700.00	$121,354,200.00
Fulfillment G & A	($7,354,800.00)	($9,193,500.00)	($11,032,200.00)	($12,870,900.00)	($40,451,400.00)
EBITDA Net Income	$14,709,600.00	$18,387,000.00	$22,064,400.00	$25,741,800.00	$80,902,800.00

Compounding Revenues

Year One

	First Quarter	Second Quarter	Third Quarter	Fourth Quarter	Total
New Stores Added	0	0	0	180	180
Rx Total Revenues	$0.00	$0.00	$0.00	$1,080,000.00	$1,080,000.00
Cost of Sales	$0.00	$0.00	$0.00	($475,200.00)	($475,200.00)
Gross Profit	$0.00	$0.00	$0.00	$604,800.00	$604,800.00
Distribution to Store	$0.00	$0.00	$0.00	($151,200.00)	($151,200.00)
Sales & Marketing Costs	$0.00	$0.00	$0.00	($900,000.00)	($900,000.00)
Net Operating Income	$0.00	$0.00	$0.00	($446,400.00)	($446,400.00)

Year Two

	First Quarter	Second Quarter	Third Quarter	Fourth Quarter	Total
New Stores Added	180	360	360	360	1440
Rx Total Revenues	$2,700,000.00	$5,940,000.00	$10,800,000.00	$16,200,000.00	$35,640,000.00
Cost of Sales	($1,188,000.00)	($2,613,600.00)	($4,752,000.00)	($7,128,000.00)	($15,681,600.00)
Gross Profit	$1,512,000.00	$3,326,400.00	$6,048,000.00	$9,072,000.00	$19,958,400.00
Distribution to Store	($378,000.00)	($831,600.00)	($1,512,000.00)	($2,268,000.00)	($4,989,600.00)
Sales & Marketing Costs	($900,000.00)	($1,800,000.00)	($1,800,000.00)	($1,800,000.00)	($6,300,000.00)
Net Operating Income	$234,000.00	$694,800.00	$2,736,000.00	$5,004,000.00	$8,668,800.00

Year Three

	First Quarter	Second Quarter	Third Quarter	Fourth Quarter	Total
New Stores Added	360	360	360	360	2880
Rx Total Revenues	$22,680,000.00	$25,920,000.00	$35,640,000.00	$42,120,000.00	$126,360,000.00
Cost of Sales	($9,979,200.00)	($11,404,800.00)	($15,681,600.00)	($18,532,800.00)	($55,598,400.00)
Gross Profit	$12,700,800.00	$14,515,200.00	$19,958,400.00	$23,587,200.00	$70,761,600.00
Distribution to Store	($3,175,200.00)	($3,628,800.00)	($4,989,600.00)	($5,896,800.00)	($17,690,400.00)
Sales & Marketing Costs	($1,800,000.00)	($1,800,000.00)	($1,800,000.00)	($1,800,000.00)	($7,200,000.00)
Net Operating Income	$7,725,600.00	$9,086,400.00	$13,168,800.00	$15,890,400.00	$45,871,200.00

Retail Revenues

Year One

	First Quarter	Second Quarter	Third Quarter	Fourth Quarter	Total
New Stores Added	0	0	0	300	300
Rx per Store	0	0	0	864	1,728
Total Rx	0	0	0	259,200	259,200
Single Store Revenue	$0.00	$0.00	$0.00	$1,641.60	$1,641.60
Net Revenue EBITDA	$0.00	$0.00	$0.00	$492,480.00	$492,480.00
Total Rx Sales	$0.00	$0.00	$0.00	$9,849,600.00	$9,849,600.00

Year Two

	First Quarter	Second Quarter	Third Quarter	Fourth Quarter	Total
New Stores Added	300	300	300	300	1500
Rx per Store	864	864	1,296	1,296	4,320
Total Rx	518,400	777,600	1,036,800	1,425,600	3,758,400
Single Store Revenue	$1,641.60	$1,641.60	$2,462.40	$2,462.40	$8,208.00
Net Revenue EBITDA	$984,960.00	$1,477,440.00	$1,969,920.00	$2,708,640.00	$7,140,960.00
Total Rx Sales	$19,699,200.00	$29,548,800.00	$39,398,400.00	$54,172,800.00	$142,819,200.00

Year Three

	First Quarter	Second Quarter	Third Quarter	Fourth Quarter	Total
New Stores Added	300	300	300	300	2700
Rx per Store	1,296	1,296	1,728	1,728	6,048
Total Rx	1,555,200	1,814,400	2,073,600	2,592,000	8,035,200
Single Store Revenue	$2,462.40	$2,462.40	$3,283.20	$3,283.20	$11,491.20
Net Revenue EBITDA	$2,954,880.00	$3,447,360.00	$3,939,840.00	$4,924,800.00	$15,266,880.00
Total Rx Sales	$59,097,600.00	$68,947,200.00	$78,796,800.00	$98,496,000.00	$305,337,600.00

CHSI

(000's Omitted)

Valuation of Company: EBITDA Multiple

Value at Cash Flow Multiple	8.00	1,032,899
(Equivalent P/E)	14.77	
Less:		
Outstanding (Debt) Cash		(9,009)
Net Common Value		1,023,891
Management	70.00%	716,723
Equity Partner	30.00%	307,167

	Yr 0	Year 1	Year 2	Year 3
Management				
Investment at Market Rate Today	(1,942)			
Mgmt Fee & Guarantee Pay		-	-	-
Preferred Distributions		-	-	-
Equity Participation		-	-	716,723
Total Cash on Cash	(1,942)	-	-	716,723
Investment IRR %	617.30%			
Equity Partner				
Investment	(12,000)			
Equity Participation		-	-	307,167
Total Cash on Cash	(12,000)	-	-	307,167
Investment IRR %	194.71%			

March Financials

4/14/00

CHSI
(000's Omitted)

Alternative Valuation:
Discounted Cash Flows - After Tax

	Yr 0	Year 1	Year 2	Year 3
Pretax Income		(4,739)	25,816	115,510
Taxes		(1,896)	10,326	46,204
After Tax Income		(2,844)	15,490	69,306
Add: Depreciation/Amort		1,895	7,174	11,390
Less: Capital Expenditures		(9,700)	(29,800)	(23,800)
Less: Changes in W.C.		(1,163)	(30,952)	(60,167)
After Tax Cash Flows		(11,811)	(38,088)	(3,271)

Discount Rate (After Tax)	15.00%	15.50%	16.00%	16.50%	17.00%	17.50%
Discount Rate (Pre Tax)	24.67%	25.49%	26.32%	27.14%	27.95%	28.78%
Cash Flow in Year 3	(3,271)	(3,271)	(3,271)	(3,271)	(3,271)	(3,271)
Divided by Discount Rate	15.00%	15.50%	16.00%	16.50%	17.00%	17.50%
Residual Value of Company	(21,804)	(21,100)	(20,441)	(19,821)	(19,238)	(18,689)
Present Value of Residual	(14,336)	(13,694)	(13,096)	(12,536)	(12,012)	(11,520)
Present Value of Cash Flows	(41,221)	(40,900)	(40,583)	(40,270)	(39,961)	(39,655)
Equity Value	(55,557)	(54,594)	(53,678)	(52,806)	(51,973)	(51,176)

4/14/00

Small Business Administration Loan Forms

SMALL BUSINESS ADMINISTRATION

CHECK LIST OF REQUIRED PAPERS TO BE OBTAINED FROM APPLICANTS SBA/BANK FINANCING.

1. Application for Loan: SBA form 4, 4l

2. Statement of Personal History: SBA form 912

3. Personal Financial Statement: SBA form 413

4. Detailed, signed Balance Sheet and Profit & Loss Statements current (within 90 days of application) and last three (3) fiscal years Supplementary Schedules required on Current Financial Statements.

5. Detailed one (1) year projection of Income & Finances (please attach written explanation as to how you expect to achieve same).

6. A list of names and addresses of any subsidiaries and affiliates, including concerns in which the applicant holds a controlling (but not necessarily a majority) interest and other concerns that may be affiliated by stock ownership, franchise, proposed merger or otherwise with the applicant.

7. Certificate of Doing Business (If a corporation, stamp corporate seal on SBA form 4 section 12).

8. By Law, the Agency may not guarantee a loan if a business can obtain funds on reasonable terms from a bank or other private source. A borrower therefore must first seek private financing.

   A company must be independently owned and operated, not dominant in its field and must meet certain standards of size in terms of employees or annual receipts. Loans cannot b made to speculative businesses, newspapers, or businesses engaged in gambling.

   Applicants for loans must also agree to comply with SBA regulation that there will be no discrimination in employment or services to the public, based on race, color, religion, national origin, sex or marital status.

9. Signed Business Federal Income Tax Returns for previous three (3) year.

10. Signed Personal Federal Income Tax Returns of principals for previous three (3) years.

11. Personal Resume including business experience of each principal.

12. Brief history of the business and its problems:
Include an explanation of why the SBA loan is needed and how it will help the business.

13. Copy of Business Lease (or note from landlord giving terms of proposed lease.

14. For purchase of an existing business:
    a. Current Balance Sheet and Profit & Loss Statement of business to be purchased.
    b. Previous two (2) years Federal Income Tax Returns of the business.
    c. Propose Bill of Sale Including: Terms of Sale.
    d. Asking Price with schedule of:
        1. Inventory
        2. Machinery & Equipment
        3. Furniture & Fixtures

ASSET PURCHASE AGREEMENT

THIS ASSET PURCHASE AGREEMENT (the "Agreement") is made and entered into this ___ day of _____, 2005, by and among **XYZ CORPORATION**, a Delaware corporation ("Purchaser") and **JBC RETAIL, INC.,** an Illinois corporation ("Seller"). Purchaser and Seller are sometimes hereinafter referred to collectively as the "Parties" and individually as a "Party."

BACKGROUND:

A.   Seller is engaged in the business of _____ ("Seller's Business").

B.   Pursuant to the terms and conditions contained herein, Seller desires to sell to Purchaser, and Purchaser desires to purchase from Seller, all of the assets owned or used by Seller in connection with the operation of Seller's Business.

NOW, THEREFORE, FOR AND IN CONSIDERATION of the premises, the mutual promises, covenants and agreements contained herein, and other good and valuable consideration, the receipt and sufficiency of which are hereby acknowledged, the Parties hereby agree as follows:

ARTICLE 1
PURCHASE AND SALE OF ASSETS

1.1   **Transfer of Assets.** Upon the terms and subject to the conditions set forth in this Agreement, Seller hereby sells, conveys, transfers, assigns and delivers to Purchaser, and Purchaser hereby purchases from Seller, the "Assets" (as defined in this Section 1.1), free and clear of any and all liens, charges, security interests, mortgages, hypothecations, pledges, claims and encumbrances of any kind (each, a "Lien"). For purposes of this Agreement, "Assets" shall mean the following assets, properties and rights of Seller:

(a)   All inventory on hand and placed on consignment

(b)   all machinery, tools, equipment, computers, modems, servers, hardware, office equipment and supplies, service equipment and machinery, furniture, fixtures and other tangible personal property, including inventory;

(c)   all "Intellectual Property Assets" (as defined in Section 3.22 hereof) owned, held or used by Seller in connection with the operation of the Seller's Business;

(d)   to the extent assignable, all permits, licenses, franchises, registrations, approvals and authorizations from all governmental or regulatory authorities which are desirable or necessary to conduct Seller's Business;

(e)   all rights under all contracts, agreements, covenants, options, leases, guaranties, licenses, notes, loans, instruments and other similar arrangements related to Seller's Business to which Seller is a party or to which any of its assets are subject, whether oral or written, express or implied (collectively, the "Seller Contracts");

(f)   all records, files, correspondence, data plans, training materials, marketing materials,, customer lists and databases, work schedules, recorded knowledge and information used in Seller's Business or required to continue Seller's business as it is currently being conducted;

(g)   all accounts, notes and other receivables of Seller;

(h)   all prepaid rent and any prepaid security deposit in connection with any leased real property and all other prepaid expenses;

(i)   all telephone and facsimile numbers, e-mail addresses and Internet websites, domain names and addresses;

(j)   all warranty claims, other claims, causes of action, choses in action, rights or recovery, rights of set off and rights of recoupment against any person to the extent they relate to the Seller's Business, whether arising before or after the date hereof;

(k)   all goodwill associated with Seller's Business;

(l)   the names used in the business and any similar names and any logos associated therewith;

(m)   all other tangible and intangible assets of any kind or description, wherever located, that are owned or used by Seller in connection with the operation of Seller's Business, except as specifically set forth in Section 1.2.

1.2   **Excluded Assets**. Notwithstanding anything else contained herein to the contrary, all assets of Seller other than the Assets (collectively, the "Excluded Assets") are being retained by Seller and are not being sold to Purchaser pursuant to this Agreement.

1.3   **Assumed Liabilities**. Upon the terms and subject to the conditions contained herein, Seller hereby assigns to Purchaser, and Purchaser hereby assumes and agrees to perform and discharge, the liabilities and obligations of Seller (collectively, the "Assumed Liabilities") under the Seller Contracts listed on Schedule 1.3, but solely to the extent such liabilities relate to any period of time after the date hereof. Notwithstanding anything else contained herein to the contrary, Purchaser is not assuming (and shall have no obligation with respect to) any liability arising as a result of any breach of any Seller Contract by Seller at or before the date hereof.

1.4   **Excluded Liabilities**. Notwithstanding anything else contained herein to the contrary, all liabilities and obligations of Seller (whether known or unknown, liquidated or unliquidated, contingent or fixed) other than the Assumed Liabilities (collectively, the "Excluded Liabilities") shall remain the liabilities and obligations of Seller and are not being assumed by Purchaser pursuant hereto (regardless of whether any such liabilities or obligations are disclosed in this Agreement). Seller hereby agrees that it will fully and timely pay, perform and discharge all of the Excluded Liabilities in accordance with their respective terms.

1.5 **Assignment of Seller Contracts**. If any Seller Contract is not assignable or transferable either by virtue of the provisions thereof or under applicable law without the consent of a third party and such consent has not yet been obtained by Seller, this Agreement and the related instruments of transfer shall not constitute an assignment or transfer of the corresponding Seller Contract, and Purchaser shall not and does not assume Seller's obligations thereof. Instead, Seller shall use commercially reasonable efforts, and Purchaser will cooperate in connection with such efforts, to obtain any such required consents as soon as reasonably possible after the date hereof (and, upon the receipt of any such required consent, the corresponding Seller Contract shall be deemed automatically assigned and transferred to Purchaser, and Purchaser shall be deemed automatically to have assumed Seller's obligations thereunder, all as of such date and in manner consistent with the terms and conditions of this Agreement) and, in the meantime, otherwise obtain for Purchaser the practical benefit of such property or rights (and, assuming Purchaser receives the benefit thereof, Purchaser shall assume the related liability therefor consistent with the provisions of Section 1.3).

1.6 **Purchase Price**. Subject to the terms and conditions contained herein, Purchaser is paying to Seller a total purchase price for the Assets in an amount equal

ARTICLE 2
REPRESENTATIONS AND WARRANTIES
REGARDING SHAREHOLDERS

Each Shareholder hereby represents and warrants to Purchaser as follows:

2.1 **Due Execution; Binding Effect.** This Agreement, and each other certificate, agreement, document or instrument to be executed and delivered by him in connection with the transactions contemplated by this Agreement, has been duly executed and delivered by him and constitutes his legal, valid and binding obligation, enforceable against him in accordance with its terms.

2.2 **No Violation; Consents.** The execution, delivery and performance by him of this Agreement, and each other certificate, agreement, document or instrument to be executed and delivered by him in connection with the transactions contemplated by this Agreement, the consummation of the transactions contemplated hereby and thereby, and the fulfillment of and compliance with the terms and conditions hereof and thereof do not and will not, with or without the passing of time or the giving of notice, or both: (a) breach or otherwise constitute or give rise to a default under, result in the loss of any benefit under or permit the acceleration of any obligation under any contract, commitment or other obligation to or by which he is a party or is bound; (b) violate any statute, ordinance, law, rule, regulation, judgment, order or decree of any court or other governmental or regulatory authority to which he is subject; or (c) require him to make or obtain any consent, approval, order or authorization of, notice to, or filing, recording, registration or qualification with any person, entity, court or governmental or regulatory authority.

ARTICLE 3
REPRESENTATIONS AND WARRANTIES
REGARDING SELLER

To induce Purchaser to enter into this Agreement and consummate the transaction described herein (the "Transaction"), Seller and the Shareholders, jointly and severally, hereby make the following representations and warranties to Purchaser. The disclosure schedules attached hereto shall be arranged in sections and subsections corresponding to the numbered and lettered sections and subsections specifically referenced in this Article 3. The disclosures in any section or subsection of the disclosure schedules shall qualify only the corresponding section or subsection in this Article 3 and no disclosure made on a particular section or subsection of the disclosure schedules shall be deemed made on any other section or subsection unless expressly made thereon (by cross-reference or otherwise).

3.1   **Corporate Existence**. Seller is a corporation duly organized, validly existing and in corporate and tax good standing under the laws of the State of Illinois. Seller is duly qualified to do business and is in good standing as a foreign corporation in each jurisdiction where the conduct of Seller's Business by it requires it to be so qualified. Schedule 3.1 sets forth the jurisdictions in which the conduct of Seller's Business requires it to be qualified as a foreign corporation.

3.2   **Corporate Power; Authorization; Enforceable Obligations**. Seller has the corporate power, authority and legal right to execute, deliver and perform this Agreement and the other agreements, documents and instruments required to be delivered by Seller in connection with this Agreement. All agreements, documents, and instruments required to be delivered by Seller pursuant to this Agreement are sometimes collectively referred to hereinafter as the "Seller's Documents". The execution, delivery and performance by Seller of this Agreement and of Seller's Documents have been duly authorized by all necessary corporate and shareholder action on the part of Seller. This Agreement has been, and the Seller's Documents will be, duly executed and delivered on behalf of Seller by duly authorized officers of Seller, and this Agreement constitutes, and the Seller's Documents when executed and delivered will constitute, the legal, valid and binding obligations of Seller, enforceable against Seller in accordance with their respective terms.

3.3   **Validity of Contemplated Transactions, Etc**. The execution, delivery, consummation and performance of this Agreement and each of Seller's Documents by Seller does not and will not, directly or indirectly (with or without notice or lapse of time), violate, conflict with or result in the breach of any term, condition or provision of, or require the consent of any other person or entity under, (a) any existing law, ordinance, or governmental rule or regulation ("Laws") to which Seller or any of the Assets is subject, (b) any resolution adopted by the board of directors or the Shareholders, (c) any judgment, order, writ, injunction, decree or award of any court, arbitrator or governmental or regulatory official, body or authority which is applicable to Seller or any of the Assets, (d) the charter documents of, or any securities issued by, Seller, or (e) any mortgage, indenture, agreement, contract, commitment, lease, plan, Authorization (hereinafter defined in Section 3.15), or other instrument, document or understanding, oral or written, of Seller, by which Seller may have rights or by which any of the Assets may be bound or affected, or give any party with rights thereunder the right to terminate, modify, accelerate or otherwise change the existing rights or obligations of Seller. Except as aforesaid, no Authorization, approval or consent of, and no registration or filing with, any governmental or regulatory official, body or authority ("Governmental Entity") is required in connection with the execution, delivery or performance of this Agreement or any of the Seller's Documents by Seller. No Governmental Entity or other Person has the right to challenge the Transaction or to exercise any remedy or obtain any relief under any Laws to which Seller or any of the Assets may be subject. The consummation of the Transaction will not cause Purchaser any liability or obligation for the payment of any Taxes or result in the imposition or creation of any Lien upon or with respect to any of the Assets.

3.4   **No Third Party Options**. Except for this Agreement, there are no existing agreements, options, commitments or rights with, of or to any person or entity to acquire any of the Assets or any interest therein.

3.5   **Financial Statements**. Seller has delivered to Purchaser true and complete copies of the compiled balance sheets as of May 31, 2005, December 31, 2004 and December 31, 2003 and the related statements of income, changes in equity and cash flows of Seller's Business for the five months ended as of May 31, 2005, for the twelve months ended as of December 31, 2004 and for the twelve months ended as of December 31, 2003 (the "Financial Statements"), which Financial Statements are attached hereto as Schedule 3.5. All of the Financial Statements (a) have been prepared in accordance with United States generally accepted accounting principles consistently applied throughout the periods involved thereby, (b) fairly present the financial condition, results of operations and cash flows of Seller's Business as of the respective dates thereof and for the periods referred to therein, and (c) are consistent with the books and records for Seller's Business. References in this Agreement to the "Balance Sheet" shall mean the balance sheet of Seller's Business as of May 31, 2005 referred to above; and references in this Agreement to the "Balance Sheet Date" shall be deemed to refer to May 31, 2005.

3.6   **Accounts Receivable**. The accounts receivables of Seller's Business as set forth on the Balance Sheet or arising since the date thereof are valid and genuine; have arisen solely out of bona fide sales, performance of services and other business transactions in the ordinary course of business consistent with past practice (net of all applicable rebates and credits); are not subject to valid defenses, set-offs or counterclaims; and are collectible within ninety (90) days after billing at the full recorded amount thereof, net of the allowance for doubtful accounts set forth on the Balance Sheet. No portion of the accounts receivable is required or expected to be paid to any person or entity other than Seller.

3.7   **Inventory**. The parties hereto agree to hire a 3rd party inventory service firm to conduct an inventory at a time just prior to closing of the transaction. The inventory shall be calculated at net cost for purposes of calculating the purchase price for the business.

3.8   **Absence of Undisclosed Liabilities**. There are no liabilities or obligations with respect to the Assets or Seller's Business except those liabilities or obligations set forth on the Balance Sheet or incurred since the Balance Sheet Date in the normal and ordinary course of business, consistent with past business practice. For purposes of this Agreement, the term "liabilities" shall include, without limitation, any direct or indirect indebtedness, guaranty, endorsement, claim, loss, damage, deficiency, cost, expense, obligation, duty or responsibility, fixed or unfixed, known or unknown, matured or unmatured, absolute or contingent, asserted or unasserted, choate or inchoate, liquidated or unliquidated, secured or unsecured or the future performance of services for which revenue has already been received by Seller's Business.

3.9   **Outstanding Checks**. Each checking account for Seller's Business has a balance equal to or in excess of the aggregate amount of all outstanding checks and other withdrawals against such account.

3.10   **Taxes and Tax Returns**. All federal, state, local and foreign tax returns, reports, statements and other similar filings required to be filed by Seller in connection with Seller's Business (the "Tax Returns") with respect to any federal, state, local or foreign taxes, assessments, interest, penalties, deficiencies, fees and other governmental charges or impositions (including without limitation all income tax, unemployment compensation, social security, payroll, sales and use, excise, privilege, property, ad valorem, franchise, license, school and any other tax or similar governmental charge or imposition under laws of the United States or any state or political subdivision thereof or any foreign country or political subdivision thereof) (the "Taxes"), have been timely filed with the appropriate governmental agencies in all jurisdictions in which such Tax Returns are required to be filed and all such Tax Returns properly reflect the liabilities of Seller with respect to Seller's Business for Taxes for the periods, property or events covered thereby. All Taxes, including without limitation those which are called for by the Tax Returns or heretofore or hereafter claimed to be due by any taxing authority from Seller have been properly accrued or paid and the amount of accruals for Taxes recorded on the books of Seller's Business is adequate to cover the Tax liabilities of Seller with respect to Seller's Business. Seller has not received any notice of assessment or proposed assessment in connection with any Tax Returns relating to Seller's Business and there are no pending tax examinations of or tax claims asserted against Seller in connection with Seller's Business or any of the Assets. Seller has not been informed by any jurisdiction that the jurisdiction believes that Seller was required to file any Tax Return with respect to Seller's Business that was not filed. Seller has not extended, or waived the application of, any statute of limitations of any jurisdiction regarding the assessment or collection of any Taxes of Seller's Business nor has Seller executed or filed any power of attorney with any Taxing Authority, with respect to Seller's Business. There are no tax liens (other than any lien for current Taxes not yet due and payable) on any of the Assets. Seller has no knowledge of any basis for any additional assessment of any Taxes. All Taxes that Seller was required by Law to withhold or collect pertaining to Seller's Business have been duly withheld or collected and, to the extent required, have been properly paid to the appropriate Governmental Entity. Seller (i) has no actual or potential liability under Treasury Regulations Section 1.1502-6 (or any similar provision of federal, state, local or foreign Law), as a transferee or successor, by contract or otherwise, for any Taxes of any other person, and (ii) is not a party to or bound by any Tax indemnity, Tax sharing, Tax allocation or similar agreement. In connection with Seller's Business, Seller has not made, is not obligated to make, or is not a party to any agreement that could obligate it to make any payments that may be treated as an "excess parachute payment" under Section 280G of the Internal Revenue Code of 1986, as amended. Schedule 3.10 sets forth each jurisdiction (other than United States federal) in which a Tax Return is required to be filed by or on behalf of Seller with respect to Seller's Business, or in which Seller is or has been liable for any Taxes related to Seller's Business on a "nexus" basis.

3.11   **Books of Account**. The books, records and accounts of Seller's Business, all of which have been made available to Purchaser, are complete and correct and accurately and fairly reflect, in reasonable detail, all of the transactions and the assets and liabilities of Seller's Business and have been maintained by Seller by an adequate system of internal controls. Seller has not engaged in any transaction with respect to Seller's Business, maintained any bank account for Seller's Business or used any of the funds of Seller in the conduct of Seller's Business except for transactions, bank accounts and funds which have been and are reflected in the normally maintained books and records of Seller's Business.

3.12   **Existing Condition**. Since the Balance Sheet Date, Seller has not, with respect to Seller's Business:

(a)   incurred any liabilities, other than liabilities incurred in the ordinary course of business consistent with past practice, or discharged or satisfied any lien or encumbrance, or paid any liabilities, other than in the ordinary course of business consistent with past practice, or failed to pay or discharge when due any liabilities of which the failure to pay or discharge has caused or will cause any material damage or risk of material loss to it or any of its assets or properties;

(b)   sold, encumbered, assigned or transferred any assets or properties which would have been included in the Assets if the Transaction would have been consummated on the Balance Sheet Date or on any date since then;

(c) created, incurred, assumed or guaranteed any indebtedness for money borrowed, or mortgaged, pledged or subjected any of the Assets to any mortgage, lien, pledge, security interest, conditional sales contract or other encumbrance of any nature whatsoever, except for Permitted Liens (hereinafter defined in Section 3.13);

(d) made or suffered any amendment or termination of any material agreement, contract, commitment, lease or plan to which it is a party or by which it is bound, or canceled, modified or waived any substantial debts or claims held by it or waived any rights of substantial value, whether or not in the ordinary course of business;

(e) declared, set aside or paid any dividend or made or agreed to make any other distribution or payment in respect of its capital stock, redeemed, purchased or otherwise acquired or agreed to redeem, purchase or acquire any of its capital stock or issued or agreed to issue any of its capital stock or any options, warrants or other rights to acquire any of its capital stock;

(f) suffered any damage, destruction or loss, whether or not covered by insurance, (i) materially and adversely affecting Seller's Business, operations, assets, properties, prospects or condition (financial or otherwise) or (ii) of any item or items carried on its books of account individually or in the aggregate at more than $25,000, or suffered any repeated, recurring or prolonged shortage, cessation or interruption of supplies or utilities or other services required to conduct Seller's Business and operations;

(g) suffered any material adverse change in Seller's Business, operations, assets, properties, prospects or condition (financial or otherwise);

(h) received notice or had knowledge of any occurrence, event or condition which has had or might have a material adverse effect on Seller's Business, operations, assets, properties, prospects or condition (financial or otherwise);

(i) made commitments or agreements for capital expenditures or capital additions or betterments exceeding in the aggregate $5,000 except such as may be involved in ordinary repair, maintenance or replacement of the Assets;

(j) increased the salaries or other compensation of, or made any advance (excluding advances for ordinary and necessary business expenses) or loan to, any of its officers, directors, employees, independent contractors, consultants, affiliates or shareholders or made any increase in, or any addition to, other benefits to which any such persons may be entitled, except for annual salary increases or bonus awards to employees who are not officers or directors of Seller made in the ordinary course of business consistent with past practice;

(k)   changed any of the accounting principles followed by it or the methods of applying such principles; or

(l)   except for this Agreement, entered into any transaction other than in the ordinary course of business consistent with past practice.

3.13   **Title to Assets**. Seller has good, valid and marketable title to all of the properties and assets (real, personal and mixed) which are included in the Assets and which it purports to own, and has good leasehold title to those properties and assets it purports to lease, including without limitation all properties and assets reflected in the Balance Sheet (except for receivables collected since the date thereof in the ordinary course of business consistent with past practice), free and clear of all Liens, except for (a) any Lien for Taxes not yet due or delinquent and (b) any statutory Lien arising in the ordinary course of business by operation of Law with respect to a liability that is not yet due or delinquent (collectively, "Permitted Liens").

3.14   **Tangible Assets**. All equipment and other items of tangible property and assets which are included in the Assets are in good operating condition and repair, subject to normal wear and maintenance, are usable in the regular and ordinary course of business and conform to all applicable Laws (as defined in Section 3.15 hereof) and Authorizations relating to their use and operation. No person other than Seller owns any equipment or other items of tangible property or assets situated on the premises of Seller or which are necessary to the operation of Seller's Business, except for leased items disclosed in the disclosure schedules attached hereto.

3.15   **Compliance with Laws; Authorizations**. Seller has complied with each, and is not in violation of any, law, ordinance, governmental or regulatory rule or regulation, judgment, decision or order, whether federal, state, local or foreign, to which Seller's Business, any of the Assets or any of Seller's employees working for Seller's Business are subject, including without limitation the Health Insurance Portability and Accountability Act of 1996 (collectively, "Laws"). No event has occurred or circumstance exists that (with or without notice or lapse of time) (a) may constitute or result in a violation by Seller of, or a failure on the part of Seller to comply with, any Laws, or (b) may give rise to any obligation on the part of Seller to undertake, or to bear all or any portion of the cost of, any remedial action of any nature. Seller has not received any notice or other communication (whether oral or written) from any Governmental Entity or any other person regarding (i) any actual, alleged, possible or potential violation of, or failure to comply with, any Laws, or (ii) any actual, alleged, possible or potential obligation on the part of Seller to undertake, or to bear all or any portion of the cost of, any remedial action of any nature. Seller owns, holds, possesses and lawfully uses in the operation of Seller's Business all franchises, licenses, permits, easements, rights, applications, filings, registrations, approvals of any nature and other authorizations (collectively, "Authorizations") which are in any manner necessary for the conduct of Seller's Business as now or previously conducted or for the ownership and use of the Assets, all of which are listed and described in Schedule 3.15. Seller has delivered accurate and complete copies of all Authorizations to Purchaser. Seller is not in default, and Seller has not received any notice of any claim of default, with respect to any Authorization. No event has occurred or circumstance exists that may (with or without notice or lapse of time) (A) constitute or result directly or indirectly in a violation of or a failure to comply with any term or requirement of any Authorizations listed or required to be listed on Schedule 3.15, or (B) result directly or indirectly in the revocation, withdrawal, suspension, cancellation or termination of, or any modification to, any Authorizations listed or required to be listed on Schedule 3.15. All such Authorizations are renewable by their terms or in the ordinary course of business without the need to comply with any special qualification procedures or to pay any amounts other than routine filing fees. None of such Authorizations will be adversely affected by consummation of the Transaction. No person or entity owns or has any proprietary, financial or other interest (direct or indirect) in any Authorization which Seller owns, possesses or uses in the operation of Seller's Business.

3.16 **Litigation**. No action, hearing, suit, litigation, arbitration, investigation or other proceeding ("Proceeding") of or before any court, arbitrator or governmental or regulatory official, body or authority is pending or, to the knowledge of Seller, threatened against Seller, which relates to Seller's Business, the Assets or the Transaction, nor to the knowledge of Seller is there any reasonably likely basis for any such Proceeding, the result of which could adversely affect Seller, Seller's Business, the Assets or the Transaction. Seller is not a party to or subject to the provisions of any judgment, order, writ, injunction, decree or award of any court, arbitrator or governmental or regulatory official, body or authority which may adversely affect Seller, Seller's Business, the Assets or the Transaction.

3.17 **Insurance**. The assets, properties and operations of Seller's Business are insured under various policies of property and casualty insurance, all of which are described in Schedule 3.17, which schedule discloses (a) any and all policies covering general liability, excess liability, product liability, workers' compensation, auto liability, foreign liability, property damage, directors and officers liability, fiduciary liability, employment practices liability, professional liability, errors and omissions liability, or environmental liability of Seller or its employees, officers, directors, property, or business, and (b) for each such policy the risks insured against, insurer name, policy number, policy dates, occurrence and aggregate coverage limits, retentions and deductible amounts, premium, broker name, and whether the terms of such policy provide for retrospective premium adjustments. All such policies are in full force and effect in accordance with their terms, no notice of cancellation has been received, and there is no existing default or event which, with the giving of notice or lapse of time or both, would constitute a default thereunder. Such policies are in amounts which are adequate in relation to Seller's Business, have been in effect for the past five years, and all premiums to date have been paid in full. Schedule 3.17 also contains a true and complete description of all outstanding bonds and other surety arrangements issued or entered into in connection with Seller's Business.

3.18   **Agreements, Contracts and Commitments.** Schedule 3.18 contains an accurate list of the following agreements, contracts, commitments, leases, plans, arrangements, promises, undertakings, practices, consensual obligations and other instruments, documents and understandings (whether written or oral) which relates to Seller's Business or by which any of the Assets may be bound or affected (collectively, the "Contracts"):

(a)   any agreement, contract or commitment with any present or former shareholder, employee, officer, director, affiliate, independent contractor, consultant or advisor;

(b)   any agreement, contract or commitment for the future purchase by Seller of products or services which involves $5,000 or more or containing minimum purchase conditions or requirements or other terms that restrict or limit the purchasing relationships of Seller or its affiliates;

(c)   any agreement that was not entered into in the ordinary course of business;

(d)   any agreement, contract or commitment by Seller's Business to sell or supply products or to perform services which involves $5,000 or more or which relates to any warranty provided by Seller (with respect to Seller's Business);

(e)   any distribution, dealer, partnership, joint venture, representative, sales agency or similar agreement, contract or commitment;

(f)   any lease under which Seller is either a lessor or lessee with respect to the Assets or relating to any real property at which any of the Assets are located;

(g)   any note, debenture, bond, equipment trust agreement, letter of credit agreement, loan agreement or other agreement, contract or commitment for the borrowing or lending of money or any guarantee, pledge or undertaking of the indebtedness of any other person or entity and any deed, mortgage, lien or other encumbrance affecting any of the Assets;

(h)   any agreement, contract or commitment for any capital expenditure or leasehold improvement in excess of $5,000;

(i)   any agreement, contract or commitment containing covenants (i) purporting to limit or restrain Seller or any employee or manager of Seller, from engaging or competing in any manner or in any business in any geographic area with Seller's Business, from disclosing any confidential information of Seller's Business, from misappropriating any trade secrets of Seller's Business or that contains any nonsolicitation provisions with respect to Seller's Business or (ii) requiring Seller to deal exclusively with, grant exclusive rights to or refrain from dealing with products competitive with the products of any customer, vendor, supplier, distributor, contractor or other party with respect to Seller's Business;

(j)   any license, franchise, computer service, distributorship or other agreement which relates in whole or in part to any Intellectual Property Asset;

(k)   any other agreement, contract or commitment relating to Seller's Business not otherwise listed on Schedule 3.18 and which either (i) continues over a period of more than six months from the date hereof, (ii) exceeds $5,000 in value, (iii) is otherwise material to Seller's Business or the Assets or (iv) contains termination or other provisions triggered by the Transaction;

(l)   all of the Seller Contracts; and

(m)   all outstanding offers or solicitations made by or to Seller to enter into any of the foregoing with regard to the operation of Seller's Business.

Seller has delivered to Purchaser complete and accurate copies of each Contract. Each Contract is valid and enforceable against the parties thereto in accordance with its terms. With regard to each Contract to which Seller is a party, Seller is, and to the knowledge of Seller, all other parties thereto are, in compliance with the provisions thereof; Seller is not, and to the knowledge of Seller, no other party thereto is, in default in the performance, observance or fulfillment of any obligation, covenant or condition contained therein; and no event has occurred, is pending or is threatened, which with or without the giving of notice or lapse of time, or both, would constitute a default thereunder. Each Contract which is being assigned to or assumed by Purchaser (each, an "Assumed Contract") is listed on Schedule 3.18 and is assignable by Seller to Purchaser and except as set forth and described in Schedule 3.18, no Assumed Contract requires consent of any party to its assignment in connection with the Transaction.

3.19   **Employee Benefit Plans and Labor Matters**.

(a)   Schedule 3.19 contains a complete list of all employee benefit plans, programs, policies, practices, and other arrangements providing benefits to any employee or former employee or beneficiary or dependent thereof, whether formal or informal, whether or not set forth in writing, and whether covering one person or more than one person, sponsored or maintained or contributed to, or required to be contributed to, by Seller with respect to Seller's Business ("Plans"). With respect to each Plan, Seller has made available to Purchaser a true, correct and complete copy of (i) each writing constituting a part of such Plan, including all plan documents and amendments thereto, benefit schedules, trust agreements, and insurance contracts and other funding vehicles; (ii) the three most recent Annual Reports (Form 5500 Series) and accompanying schedules, if any; (iii) the current summary plan description, if any; (iv) the most recent annual financial report, if any; (v) the most recent determination letter from the Internal Revenue

Service, if any; (vi) the most recent actuarial/valuation, if any; and (vii) any notices provided either to any participants in any Plan or to any governmental agency, commission or regulatory body relative to any Plan in the past five years.

(b) Seller does not maintain any Plan that is intended to be a "qualified plan" within the meaning of Section 401(a) of the Code in connection with the operation of Seller's Business. Seller and all entities who is in the same controlled group of corporations or who is under common control with Seller within the meaning of Section 414 of the Code ("ERISA Affiliates") have complied and are in compliance with all provisions of the Employee Retirement Income Security Act of 1974 ("ERISA"), the Code and all Laws applicable to the Plans. Each Plan has been operated in compliance with its terms and in accordance with all applicable Laws. There is not now, and here are no existing, circumstances that could give rise to any requirement for the posting of security with respect to a Plan or the imposition of any Lien on the Assets under ERISA or the Code.

(c) No Plan is subject to Title IV or Section 302 of ERISA or Section 412 or 4971 of the Code. No Plan is a "multiemployer plan" within the meaning of Section 4001(a)(3) of ERISA ("Multiemployer Plan") or a plan that has two or more contributing sponsors at least two of whom are not under common control, within the meaning of Section 4063 of ERISA (a "Multiple Employer Plan"), nor has Seller or any ERISA Affiliate, at any time within five years before the date hereof, contribute to or been obligated to contribute to any Multiemployer Plan or Multiple Employer Plan.

(d) Full payment has been made of all amounts that are required under the terms of each Plan to be paid as contributions with respect to all periods prior to and including the last day of the most recent fiscal year of such Plan ended on or before the date of this Agreement and all periods thereafter prior to the date hereof. Seller has paid in full all required insurance premiums, subject only to normal retrospective adjustments in the ordinary course, with regard to Plans for all policy years or other applicable policy periods ending on or before the date hereof.

(e) There does not now exist, and there are no existing, circumstances that could result in, any liability under Title IV of ERISA, Section 302 of ERISA, Sections 412 and 4971 of the Code, the continuation-coverage requirements of Sections 601 et seq. of ERISA and Section 4980B of the Code and the portability and nondiscrimination requirements of Section s 701 et seq. of ERISA and Sections 9801 et seq. of the Code, Section 4975 of the Code and corresponding or similar Laws, in each case other than pursuant to the Plans, for Purchaser following the date hereof. Without limiting the generality of the foregoing, neither Seller nor any ERISA Affiliate has engaged in any transaction described in Section 4069 of ERISA or any transaction that constitutes a withdrawal under Section 4201 et seq. of ERISA.

(f)   Seller has, at all times, complied, and currently complies, with the applicable continuation requirements for its welfare benefit plans relating to Selller's Business, including (i) Section 4980B of the Code (as well as its predecessor provision, Section 162(k) of the Code) and Sections 601 through 608, inclusive, of ERISA, which provisions are hereinafter referred to collectively as "COBRA" and (ii) any applicable state statutes mandating health insurance continuation coverage for employees.

(g)   The Transaction will not result in an amendment, modification or termination of any of the Plans. No written or oral representations have been made to any employee or former employee of Seller with respect to Seller's Business promising or guaranteeing any employer payment or funding for the continuation of medial, dental, life or disability coverage for any period of time (except to the extent of coverage required under COBRA). No written or oral representations have been made to any employee or former employee of Seller with respect to Seller's Business concerning the employee benefits of Purchaser.

(h)   Neither the execution and delivery of this Agreement nor the consummation of the Transaction will result in, cause the accelerated vesting or delivery of, or increase the amount or value of, any payment or benefit to any employee, officer, director or consultant of Seller with respect to Seller's Business. Without limiting the generality of the foregoing, no amount paid or payable by Seller in connection with the Transaction either solely as a result thereof or as a result of such transactions in conjunction with any other events will be an "excess parachute payment" within the meaning of Section 280G of the Code.

(i)   Seller is not a party to any collective bargaining agreement or any other agreement which determines the terms and conditions of employment of any employee of Seller with respect to Seller's Business. No collective bargaining agent has been certified as a representative of any of the employees of Seller with respect to Seller's Business and no representation campaign or election is now in progress with respect to any of the employees of Seller with respect to Seller's Business. Seller has not suffered any strike, slowdown, picketing or work stoppage by any union or other group of employees affecting the Business; and to the knowledge of Seller, there are no efforts underway or threats to effect any of same.

3.20   **Trade Relations**. There exists no actual or, to the knowledge of Seller, threatened termination, cancellation or limitation of, or any adverse modification or change in, the business or business relationship with any customer, pharmacist advisor, reseller or distributor with respect to Seller's Business or with any supplier of Seller's Business, and there exists no present condition or state of facts or circumstances that would adversely affect Seller's Business or prevent Purchaser from conducting Seller's Business or having business relationships with any such customer, pharmacist advisor, reseller or distributor of Seller's Business in the same manner as heretofore conducted by Seller.

3.21   **Intellectual Property.**

(a)   The term "Intellectual Property Assets" means all intellectual property owned by or licensed by or to (as licensor or licensee) Seller with respect to Seller's Business, including (i) Seller's name, all assumed fictional business names, trade names, registered and unregistered trademarks, service marks and applications relative to Seller's Business and/or Seller (collectively, "Marks"), common law trademarks and servicemarks, trade dress and all goodwill in the foregoing; (ii) all registered and unregistered copyrights in both published works and unpublished works (collectively, "Copyrights"); (iii) all rights in mask works and registrations and applications for registration thereof; (iv) all know-how, trade secrets, confidential or proprietary information, customer lists, computer software code, applications, utilities, development tools, diagnostics, databases and embedded systems, whether in source code, interpreted code or object code form (collectively, "Software"), methods, formulations, technical information, data, database rights, process technology, plans, drawings, blueprints and registrations and applications for registration of the foregoing (collectively, "Trade Secrets"); and (v) all rights in internet web sites and internet domain names presently used by Seller in Seller's Business (collectively, "Net Names"). The Intellectual Property Assets are all that is necessary for the operation of Seller's Business as it is currently conducted. There are no patents, patent applications and inventions and discoveries that may be patentable, utility models and design registrations, or certificates of invention (including all related continuations, continuations-in-part, divisionals, reissuances and reexaminations) owned by or licensed by or to Seller with respect to Seller's Business.

(b)   Schedule 3.22(b) lists all Marks, registered copyrights, registered Net Names and mask work registrations ("Intellectual Property Registrations") that are registered or filed in the name of Seller, alone or jointly with others, enumerating specifically the applicable filing or registration number, title, jurisdiction, date of filing or issuance, and status of any required issuance, renewal, maintenance or other payments. All assignments of Intellectual Property Registrations have been properly executed and recorded. Seller has delivered complete and accurate copies of all Intellectual Property Registrations to Purchaser, together with all assignments thereof. All Intellectual Property Registrations are valid and enforceable and all issuance, renewal, maintenance and other payments that are or have become due with respect thereto have been timely paid by or on behalf of Seller. To Seller's knowledge, there is no information which would preclude Seller from having clear title to the Intellectual Property Registrations or regarding the enforceability of any Intellectual Property Registrations.

(c)   Each item of Intellectual Property Assets that is either owned by or licensed to Seller will be owned or available for use by Purchaser immediately following the date hereof on substantially identical terms and conditions as it was immediately prior to the date hereof and the Intellectual Property Assets are all that is necessary for the operation of Seller's Business as it is currently being conducted by Seller. All of the Intellectual Property Assets are free and clear of all liens, claims, charges or encumbrances and Seller has the right to use such Intellectual Property Assets as they are currently used in Seller's Business without payment to a third party other than in respect of licenses listed in Schedule 3.21. None of the Intellectual Property Assets that are owned by or licensed to Seller are subject to any outstanding order, and no Proceedings are pending, or to the knowledge of Seller, threatened, which challenges the validity, enforceability, ownership, use or licensing of such Intellectual Property Assets. No shareholder, or other present or former equity owner, director or employee of Seller, and no person owns or has any proprietary, financial or other interest, direct or indirect, in any of the Intellectual Property Assets that are owned by Seller. Seller is not and to Seller's knowledge, no other person is infringing, violating or misappropriating any of the Intellectual Property Assets. Seller has provided to Purchaser copies of all correspondence, memoranda, complaints, claims, notices or threats in the possession or control of Seller or any of its affiliates and any legal opinions concerning the infringement, violation or misappropriation of any Intellectual Property Assets that are owned by Seller.

(d)   Schedule 3.21(d) contains a complete and accurate list and summary description of all Intellectual Property Assets, including any royalties payable with respect to the Intellectual Property Assets. Seller holds and possesses all of the licenses for Software which are necessary for the conduct of Seller's Business or for the ownership and use of the Assets, all of which are listed and described on Schedule 3.21(d). Seller is not in default, and Seller has not received any notice of any claim of default, with respect to any such Software license. No event has occurred or circumstance exists that may (with or without notice or lapse of time) (i) constitute or result directly or indirectly in a violation of or a failure to comply with any term or requirement of any Software license listed or required to be listed on Schedule 3.21(d). All such Software licenses are perpetual or renewable by their terms without the need to comply with any special qualification procedures or to pay any amounts. None of the Software licenses will be adversely affected by consummation of the Transaction. Except as described in Schedule 3.21(d), Seller has not agreed to indemnify any person or entity against any infringement, violation or misappropriation of any Intellectual Property Assets or any rights therein. No third party inventions, methods, services, materials, processes or Software are included in or required to use, operate, distribute or provide the services provided by Seller, except as specifically set forth in Schedule 3.21(d). None of the Software used to provide the services provided by Seller includes "shareware", "freeware" or other code that was developed by third parties for or on behalf of Seller other than as specifically set forth in Schedule 3.21(d).

(e)   Seller has not licensed, distributed or disclosed, and knows of no distribution or disclosure by others (including by any of Seller's affiliates) of, the source code for any Software used in providing the services provided by Seller, or

Microsoft Access report writing methodologies used for analyzing data, or other confidential information of Seller pertaining to Seller's Business constituting, embodied in or pertaining to such Software ("Business Source Code") to any person or entity and Seller has taken reasonable physical and electronic security measures to prevent disclosure of such Business Source Code. No event has occurred, and no circumstance or condition exists, that (with or without notice or lapse of time or both) will, or would reasonably be expected to, nor will the consummation of the Transaction, result in the disclosure or release of such Business Source Code by Seller or any escrow agent(s) or any other person or entity.

(f)   All of the Software used in providing the services provided by Seller is licensed from third parties and none of the Software used in providing such services has been modified or altered in any way from its original format as received pursuant to the Software licenses set forth in Schedule 3.21(d). Pursuant to the Software licenses set forth in Schedule 3.21(d), Seller has the appropriate use restrictions, type and number of licenses for all the Software necessary for the operation of Seller's Business as it is currently being conducted by Seller.

(g)   No Open Source Materials (defined below) are currently utilized in any way by Seller in Seller's Business. The term "Open Source Materials" means all Software that is distributed as "free software", "open source software", or under a similar licensing or distribution model, including, but not limited to, the GNU General Public License, GNU Lesser General Public License, Mozilla Public License, BSD Licenses, the Artistic License, the Netscape Public License, the Sun Community Source License, the Sun Industry Standards License and the Apache License.

(h)   Each employee of Seller (with respect to Seller's Business) and each current and former independent contractor of Seller engaged to work on one or more projects for Seller's Business has executed valid and binding written agreements expressly assigning to Seller all right, title and interest in and to any inventions and works of authorship, whether or not patentable, invented, created, developed, conceived, and/or reduced to practice during the term of such employee's employment or such independent contractor's work for Seller and all rights in any Intellectual Property Assets, and has waived all moral rights therein to the extent legally permissible.

(i)   Seller has taken all reasonable precautions to protect the proprietary nature of each item of owned Intellectual Property Assets, and to maintain in confidence all trade secrets and confidential information of Seller's Business comprising a part thereof. All employees of Seller and consultants having access to confidential information of Seller's Business have executed nondisclosure agreements, full and complete copies of which have been provided to Purchaser.

3.22   **Environmental Matters**.

(a)   Except as set forth in Schedule 3.22, Seller has obtained and holds all permits, licenses and other Authorizations under Laws relating to pollution or protection of the environment, including Laws relating to emissions, discharges, releases or threatened releases of pollutants, contaminants, chemicals, or industrial, toxic or hazardous substances or wastes into the environment (including without limitation ambient air, surface water, groundwater, or land), or otherwise relating to the manufacture, processing, distribution, use, treatment, storage, disposal, transport, or handling of pollutants, contaminants, chemicals, or industrial, toxic or hazardous substances or wastes (collectively, "Environmental Laws").

(b)   Each of Seller and its affiliates, with respect to Seller's Business, is in full compliance with, and has at all times complied with all applicable Environmental Laws and all terms and conditions of the permits, licenses and other Authorizations issued under Environmental Laws, and Seller and its affiliates also is in full compliance with, and has at all times complied with, all other limitations, restrictions, conditions, standards, prohibitions, requirements, obligations, schedules and timetables contained in Environmental Laws or contained in any order, decree, judgment, injunction, notice or demand letter issued, entered, promulgated or approved thereunder. Except as set forth in Schedule 3.22, there is no civil, criminal or administrative claim, action, demand, suit, proceeding, study or investigation pending or, to the knowledge of Seller, threatened against Seller or any of its affiliates relating to Environmental Laws. Seller has provided Purchaser with a complete and accurate copy of any and all environmental reports, investigations and audits relating to the premises currently or previously owned or operated in connection with Seller's Business (whether conducted by or on behalf of Seller or a third party).

(c)   Except as set forth in Schedule 3.22, neither Seller nor any of its affiliates has knowledge or has received notice of any past, present or future events, conditions, circumstances, activities, practices, incidents, actions or plans which may interfere with or prevent compliance or continued compliance by Seller or Seller's Business with any Environmental Laws or any order, decree, judgment, injunction, notice or demand letter issued, entered, promulgated or approved thereunder or which may give rise to any common law or legal liability, or otherwise form the basis of any claim, action, demand, suit, proceeding, hearing, study or investigation, based on or related to the manufacture, processing, distribution, use, treatment, storage, disposal, transport, or handling, or the emission, discharge, release or threatened release into the environment, of any pollutant, contaminant, chemical, or industrial, toxic or hazardous substance or waste. There is no asbestos in any friable and damaged form or condition or not in compliance with Environmental Laws contained in or forming any part of any building or structure currently or previously leased by Seller (or by any person whose liability Seller has retained or assumed either contractually or by operation of Law). There are no underground or aboveground storage tanks located on property leased by Seller or its affiliates with respect to Seller's Business.

3.24   **Purchased Assets**. The Assets include all of the business operations, assets, properties and other rights necessary for the conduct of Seller's Business by Purchaser in the manner it is presently conducted by Seller and none of the Excluded Assets, individually or collectively, constitutes business operations, assets, properties or other rights which are used in the operation of Seller's Business.

3.25   **Restrictions**. Seller is not a party to any Assumed Contract, Authorization, judgment, order, writ, injunction, decree or award which materially and adversely affects or, so far as Seller can now reasonably foresee, may in the future materially and adversely affect, the business operations, assets, properties, prospects or condition (financial or otherwise) of Seller's Business after consummation of the Transaction.

3.26   **Completeness of Disclosure**. No representation or warranty by Seller in this Agreement nor in any disclosure schedule, certificate, statement, document or instrument furnished or to be furnished to Purchaser pursuant hereto, or in connection with the negotiation, execution or performance of this Agreement, contains or will contain any untrue statement of a material fact or omits or will omit to state a material fact required to be stated herein or therein or necessary to make any statement herein or therein not misleading.

ARTICLE 4
REPRESENTATIONS AND WARRANTIES OF PURCHASER

Purchaser hereby represents and warrants to Seller and Shareholders as follows:

4.1   **Organization and Good Standing.** Purchaser is a corporation duly organized, validly existing and in good standing under the laws of the State of Delaware.

4.2   **Power and Authority.** Purchaser has the requisite corporate power and authority to enter into this Agreement, to perform its obligations hereunder and to consummate the transactions contemplated hereby. The execution and delivery of this Agreement and the consummation of the transactions contemplated hereby have been duly authorized by all necessary corporate action on the part of Purchaser.

4.3   **Due Execution; Binding Effect.** This Agreement, and each other certificate, agreement, document or instrument to be executed and delivered by Purchaser in connection with the transactions contemplated by this Agreement, has been duly executed and delivered by Purchaser and constitutes the legal, valid and binding obligation of Purchaser, enforceable against Purchaser in accordance with its terms.

4.4   **No Violation; Consents.** The execution, delivery and performance by Purchaser of this Agreement, and each other certificate, agreement, document or instrument to be executed and delivered by it in connection with the transactions contemplated by this Agreement, the consummation of the transactions contemplated hereby and thereby, and the fulfillment of and compliance with the terms and conditions hereof and thereof do not and will not, with or without the passing of time or the giving of notice, or both: (a) violate or conflict with any provision of the Certificate of Incorporation or Bylaws of Purchaser; (b) breach or otherwise constitute or give rise to a default under, result in the loss of any benefit under or permit the acceleration of any obligation under any contract, commitment or other obligation to or by which Purchaser is a party or is bound; (c) violate any statute, ordinance, law, rule, regulation, judgment, order or decree of any court or other governmental or regulatory authority to which Purchaser is subject; or (d) require Purchaser to make or obtain any consent, approval or authorization of, notice to, or filing, recording, registration or qualification with any third party, court or governmental or regulatory authority.

ARTICLE 5
OTHER AGREEMENTS OF THE PARTIES

5.1   **Brokers; Expenses.** Each Party hereto hereby represents and warrants to each other Party that it has not incurred any liability for brokerage fees, finder's fees, agent's commissions or other similar forms of compensation in connection with or in any way related to the transactions contemplated by this Agreement. Each Party hereto shall pay its own fees and expenses (including the fees and expenses of its attorneys, accountants, investment bankers, brokers, financial advisors and other professionals) incurred in connection with this Agreement and all transactions contemplated hereby.

5.2   **Publicity.** No Party shall issue any press release, written public statement or announcement relating to this Agreement or the transactions contemplated hereby without the written prior approval of the other Parties in each instance, except to the extent such disclosure is required by law (in which case such Party shall use all reasonable efforts to give the other Parties prior notice thereof).

5.3   **Confidentiality.** Seller and each Shareholder covenants and agrees that he will not, without the prior written consent of Purchaser, use, copy, disclose or otherwise distribute to any other person or entity: (a) any "Confidential Information" (as hereinafter defined) for a period of five (5) years following the date hereof; or (b) any "Trade Secrets" (as hereinafter defined) at any time such information constitutes a trade secret under applicable law. For purposes of this Section 5.3, the following terms shall have the following respective meanings:

(a)   "Confidential Information" means all valuable, proprietary and confidential business information of Purchaser that does not constitute a Trade Secret and that is not generally known by Purchaser's competitors, including, without limitation, all confidential business information of Seller that is being purchased by Purchaser as part of the Assets.

(b)   "Trade Secrets" means the trade secrets of Purchaser as defined under applicable law, including, without limitation, the trade secrets of Seller that are being purchased by Purchaser as part of the Assets.

5.4   **Non-Competition and Non-Solicitation**.

(a)   Seller and each Shareholder covenant and agree that, in consideration of the consummation of the transactions by Purchaser hereunder, neither it nor any of its affiliates, directly or indirectly, shall for a period of five (5) years after the date hereof:

(i)   engage, whether wholly or partly, in the business of _____ (the "Restricted Business") in _____ (the "Restricted Territory");

(ii)   serve as a director, officer, employee, consultant, lender, advisor, independent contractor or joint venturer with respect to an entity that wholly or partly, directly or indirectly, engages in the Restricted Business in the Restricted Territory;

(iii)   directly or indirectly own any equity interest in (excluding ownership of less than one percent (1%) of the outstanding common stock of any publicly held corporation), or control any portion of a business that wholly or partly, directly or indirectly, engages in the Restricted Business in the Restricted Territory; or

(iv)   take any action that is designed or intended to have the effect of discouraging any customer, supplier or lessor of Seller from maintaining the same business relationship with Purchaser after the date hereof as it maintained with Seller prior to the date hereof.

(b)   Seller and each Shareholder covenants and agrees that, in consideration of the consummation of the transactions by Purchaser hereunder, neither it nor any of its affiliates, employees, directors or partners, directly or indirectly, shall for a period of two (2) years from the date hereof (i) solicit, persuade or encourage any employee then employed by Purchaser or its affiliates or subsidiaries to cease employment with or retention by the Purchaser or its affiliates or subsidiaries; or (ii) hire any employee then employed by Purchaser or its affiliates or subsidiaries.

(c)   Each of Seller and each Shareholder hereby acknowledges and agrees that the covenants contained in this Section 5.4 (the "Protective Covenants") are reasonable as to time, scope and territory given Purchaser's need to protect trade secrets and confidential information, and Seller and each Shareholder acknowledges and agrees that Purchaser and its affiliates and assignees would be irreparably damaged if Seller or either Shareholder were to provide services to or otherwise participate in the Restricted Business in the Restricted Territory and that any such competition by Seller or either Shareholder would result in a significant loss of goodwill by Purchaser and its affiliates and assignees. In the event any Protective Covenant in this Agreement shall be determined by any court of competent jurisdiction to be unenforceable by reason of its extending for too great a period of time or over too great a geographical area or by reason of its being too extensive in any other respect, it shall be interpreted to extend only over the maximum period of time for which it may be enforceable and/or over the maximum geographical area as to which it may be enforceable and/or to the maximum extent in all other respects as to which it may be enforceable, all as determined by such court in such action.

(d)   Each of Seller and each Shareholder hereby acknowledges and agrees that any breach of a Protective Covenant by it will cause irreparable damage to Purchaser, the exact amount of which will be difficult to determine, and that the remedies at law for any breach will be inadequate. Accordingly, Seller and each Shareholder hereby agrees that, in addition to any other remedy that may be available at law, in equity or hereunder, the Purchaser shall be entitled to specific performance and injunctive relief without posting bond or other security, to enforce or prevent any violation of any of the Protective Covenants by it.

ARTICLE 6
INDEMNIFICATION

6.1   **Indemnification by Seller and Shareholders.** Seller and each Shareholder shall jointly and severally indemnify, promptly defend and hold harmless Purchaser and its affiliates and subsidiaries, and their respective shareholders, partners, members, employees, officers, directors, agents and representatives (collectively, the "Shareholder Indemnified Parties"), from and against any and all claims, costs, expenses (including costs of investigation, attorneys' fees and court costs), judgments, actions, suits, proceedings, penalties, fines, damages, losses and liabilities of any kind or nature (collectively, "Losses") relating to, resulting from or arising out of: (a) any breach of any representation or warranty made by Seller or either Shareholder in this Agreement; (b) any breach of any covenant or agreement of Seller or either Shareholder contained in this Agreement; (c) the Excluded Liabilities; and (d) any fraud, willful misconduct or bad faith of Seller or either Shareholder in connection with the transactions contemplated by this Agreement.

6.2   **Indemnification by Purchaser.** Purchaser shall indemnify, promptly defend and hold harmless Seller, Shareholders and their affiliates and representatives (collectively, the "Purchaser Indemnified Parties"), from and against any and all Losses relating to, resulting from or arising out of: (a) any breach of any representation or warranty made by Purchaser in this Agreement; (b) any breach of any covenant or agreement of Purchaser contained in this Agreement; (c) the Assumed Liabilities; and (d) any fraud, willful misconduct or bad faith of Purchaser in connection with the transactions contemplated by this Agreement.

6.3   **Indemnification Procedures Regarding Third Party Claims.** If any Party to this Agreement becomes aware of or receives notice of any third party claim or the commencement of any third party action or proceeding with respect to which another party (the "Indemnitor") is obligated to provide indemnification under this Article 6, the Party entitled to indemnification (the "Indemnitee") shall promptly give the Indemnitor notice thereof. Such notice shall not be a condition precedent to any liability of the Indemnitor under the provisions for indemnification contained in this Agreement, unless (and only to the extent that) failure to give such notice materially prejudices the rights of the Indemnitor with respect to such claims, actions, or proceedings. The Indemnitor may compromise or defend, at the Indemnitor's own expense, and by the Indemnitor's own counsel, any such matter involving the asserted liability of the Indemnitee; provided, however, that no compromise or settlement thereof may be effected by the Indemnitor without the Indemnitee's consent (which shall in any event not be unreasonably withheld or delayed); and further provided that an Indemnitor may not undertake the defense of any such third party claim unless (i) the claim is solely for monetary damages, and (ii) the Indemnitor confirms in writing to the Indemnitee (and to such third party), prior to undertaking such defense or prior to making such compromise or settlement, that the matter concerning indemnification is indemnifiable by the Indemnitor. If the Indemnitor elects not to compromise or defend such matter or if the Indemnitor may not undertake the defense of such third party claim, then the Indemnitee, at the Indemnitor's expense and by the Indemnitee's own counsel, may defend such matter. In any event, the Indemnitee, and the Indemnitor shall cooperate in the compromise of, or the defense against, any such asserted liability. If the Indemnitor chooses to defend any claim, the Indemnitee shall make available to the Indemnitor any books, record, or other documents within its control that are reasonably necessary or appropriate for such defense. The foregoing indemnity procedures shall not be read as a limitation on either party's right to seek indemnification under this Article 6 for matters other than third party initiated claims or demands.

6.4   **Payments.** All payments made under this Article 6 shall be deemed adjustments to the Purchase Price.

ARTICLE 7
MISCELLANEOUS

7.1   **Notices.**

(a)   All notices, consents, requests and other communications hereunder shall be in writing and shall be sent by hand delivery, by certified or registered mail (return-receipt requested), or by a recognized national overnight courier service as set forth below:

If to Purchaser: _____

_____

_____

Attention: _____

with a copy to:	_____
	_____
	_____
	Attention: _____
If to Seller:	_____
	_____
	Attention: _____
with a copy to:	_____
	_____
	Attention: _____

(b)   Notices delivered pursuant to Section 7.1(a) shall be deemed given: (i) at the time delivered, if personally delivered; (ii) at the time received, if mailed; and (iii) two (2) business days after timely delivery to the courier, if by overnight courier service.

(c)   Any Party hereto may change the address to which notice is to be sent by written notice to the other Parties in accordance with this Section 7.1.

7.2   **Entire Agreement.** This Agreement, including all schedules hereto (all of which are incorporated herein by this reference), contains the entire agreement and understanding concerning the subject matter hereof among the Parties and specifically supersedes any other agreement or understanding among the Parties related to the subject matter hereof.

7.3   **Waiver; Amendment.** No waiver, termination or discharge of this Agreement, or any of the terms or provisions hereof, shall be binding upon any Party unless confirmed in writing. No waiver by any Party of any term or provision of this Agreement or of any default hereunder shall affect such Party's rights thereafter to enforce such term or provision or to exercise any right or remedy in the event of any other default, whether or not similar. This Agreement may not be modified or amended except by a writing executed by all Parties.

7.4   **Severability.** If any provision of this Agreement shall be held void, voidable, invalid or inoperative, no other provision of this Agreement shall be affected as a result thereof, and, accordingly, the remaining provisions of this Agreement shall remain in full force and effect as though such void, voidable, invalid or inoperative provision had not been contained herein.

7.5   **Governing Law.** This Agreement shall be governed by and construed in accordance with the laws of the State of Michigan, without regard to the principles of conflicts of laws.

7.6 **Assignment.** No Party may assign this Agreement, in whole or in part, without the prior written consent of the other Parties, and any attempted assignment not in accordance herewith shall be null and void and of no force or effect.

7.7 **Binding Effect.** This Agreement shall be binding upon and shall inure to the benefit of the Parties and their respective heirs, representatives, successors and permitted assigns.

7.8 **Headings.** The titles, captions and headings contained in this Agreement are inserted for convenience of reference only and are not intended to be a part of or to affect in any way the meaning or interpretation of this Agreement.

7.9 **References within Agreement.** Numbered or lettered articles, sections, paragraphs, subsections and schedules herein contained refer to articles, sections, paragraphs, subsections, and schedules and exhibits of this Agreement unless otherwise expressly stated. The words "herein," "hereof," "hereunder," "hereby," "this Agreement" and other similar references shall be construed to mean and include this Agreement and all amendments to this Agreement unless the context shall clearly indicate or require otherwise. The word including (and all derivations thereof) shall be construed to mean "including, without limitation."

7.10 **Interpretation.** This Agreement shall not be construed more strictly against any Party regardless of which Party is responsible for its preparation.

7.11 **Further Assurances.** Upon the reasonable request of the any Party, each Party agrees to take any and all actions, necessary or appropriate to give effect to the terms and conditions set forth in this Agreement.

7.12 **Counterparts; Fax Signatures.** This Agreement may be executed in one or more counterparts, each of which shall be deemed to be an original, but all of which together shall constitute the same Agreement. Any signature page of any such counterpart, or any electronic facsimile thereof, may be attached or appended to any other counterpart to complete a fully executed counterpart of this Agreement, and any telecopy or other facsimile transmission of any signature shall be deemed an original and shall bind such Party.

IN WITNESS WHEREOF, the undersigned have executed, or have caused their respective duly authorized representatives to execute, this Agreement as of the date hereof.

"Purchaser"

XYZ Corporation

By: _____

Name: _____

Title: _____

JBC Retail, Inc.

By: _____
Name: _____
Title: _____

SCHEDULE 1.3

Assumed Liabilities

SCHEDULE 1.6

Purchase Price

Schedule 1.9

Inventory Schedule

SCHEDULE 3.6

Intellectual Property

SCHEDULE 3.7

Receivables

SCHEDULE 3.9

Litigation

SCHEDULE 3.10

Financial Statements